Heaven

Paradise is Real

Hope Beyond Death

**An Angelic Pilgrimage
to Your Future Home**

Paul Backholer

Heaven,
Paradise is Real
Hope Beyond Death
An Angelic Pilgrimage to Your Future Home
By Paul Backholer

U.K. ISBN 978-1-907066-80-1
British Library Cataloguing In Publication Data.
A Record of this Publication is available from the British Library.

First published in 2020 by ByFaith Media

- Jesus Christ is Lord -

Contents

Page   Chapter

Introduction

Heaven is the final destination for the redeemed and yet, we still have many unanswered questions about our future. What will heaven feel like? What will we look like and what did Jesus Christ mean when He taught we will be like the angels? (Matthew 22:30). The Bible does not discourage such thoughts; instead, it urges us to focus our thinking on things above. 'If then you were raised with Christ, seek those things which are above, where Christ is, sitting at the right hand of God. Set your mind on things above, not on things on the earth' (Colossians 3:1-2).

In the Old Testament, the prophets did not know the fullness of God's eternal plan, therefore Paul wrote of those generations: 'Eye has not seen, nor ear heard, nor has entered into the heart of man, the things which God has prepared for those who love Him.' But after Christ Jesus was raised from the dead and the Holy Spirit was poured out, God began to reveal His eternal destiny for His people in greater detail. Paul explained it like this: 'But God has revealed them to us through His Spirit' (1 Corinthians 2:9-10).

The apostle Paul visited the third heaven (2 Corinthians 12:2), and others have had visions and dreams; whilst the apostle John was in the Spirit when he received his visions (Revelation 1:10).

God speaks to us in His Word and the teaching of the Lord Jesus constantly refers to the afterlife – heaven and hell. His preaching insists we should weigh our actions and walk in His light as we prepare for eternity (Matthew 12:36-42, Luke 16:1-31, 21:3-37, John 10:27-28). He encouraged all to consider the next life and to live with the eternal in mind (Matthew 25:1-46). Jesus also taught that by nature we struggle to understand heaven: "If I have told you earthly things and you do not believe, how will you believe if I tell you heavenly things?" (John 3:12).

In these last days, God is pouring out the Holy Spirit and the Bible states our sons and daughters will prophesy, young men shall see visions, and old men will dream dreams (Acts 2:17). Therefore, the day of revelation is far from over; yet God will never show us anything that contradicts or challenges the authority of Scripture (John 20:31, 2 Timothy 3:16). Consequently, this chronicle may be weighed as a prophetic journal soaked in biblical truth, Divine experiences and lessons given by the Holy Spirit.

God always speaks for important reasons and believers in Jesus are told to 'desire spiritual gifts...especially that you may prophesy' (1 Corinthians 14:1). As the Bible states: 'The testimony of Jesus is the spirit of prophecy' (Revelation 19:10). We also accept that we know in part and see in part (1 Corinthians 13:12), and revelations must be tested in His light, by the Word (1 Corinthians 14:29).

As there are dangers of depending on personal revelations and man can add to and misunderstand what God gives (1 Corinthians 14:29-32), we must always return to Scripture. The Bible will always be our only and final source of doctrine, and all other aids to Scripture must be weighed in its balance. This is why this chronicle is filled with biblical references that can be sought-out and studied to corroborate the message within (2 Timothy 3:16). All you read can only be as faithful as the verses that underpin it. As Paul wrote to Timothy: 'Consider what I say and may the Lord give you understanding in all things' (2 Timothy 2:7).

I conclude this introduction by considering the prayer of the apostle Paul that we may receive revelation from God.

'...making mention of you in my prayers, that the God of our Lord Jesus Christ, the Father of glory may give you the spirit of wisdom and revelation in the knowledge of Him, the eyes of your understanding being enlightened, that you may know what is the hope of His calling, what are the riches of the glory of His inheritance in the saints' (Ephesians 1:16-18).

Chapter One

Paradise

I sometimes feel like a passenger on a high-speed train shooting through time. Where have all the years gone? I can remember school years, impatiently waiting for them to pass, so I could leave and begin my real life. But now the years go by with inconsiderate speed. In my personal battle with time, I found myself asking this question – where is this sprint through life heading?

Perhaps it is the knowledge of our mortality that helped me to study the Bible's description of heaven. When we were young, we spent our time planning in vain for a future which rarely turns out as expected. Life is the events which happen to us whilst we are making far superior plans. Nevertheless, in those precious moments between the daily routines of work, duties, burdens, commitments and responsibilities, we sometimes find a minute to stop and ponder where this mortal journey will lead.

Day after day, month after month, I opened my Bible and studied the passages of Scripture that give us a glimpse of the promise of heaven. I was amazed at the many references throughout, and the promises that provoked questions and further study. I prayed in the night hours for visions of heaven and with my spirit opened, I saw a perfect world which left me with a deep witness of heaven.

I cannot explain it all – yet, I felt I passed into another world. There was radiant light shining around me, so intense that it penetrated into my being. I knew by faith this was heaven, yet I was unable to discern where I was 'geographically.' I did not physically travel to get here and I lost my sense of coordination. Once I had thought of heaven as a physical dimension above the sky, and then I recalled the apostle John saw the sky receding like a scroll, when it rolled up before him. I concluded this was the spiritual world (Revelation 6:14).

Suddenly, a glorious shudder passed down my spine; it was not fear I felt, for I knew no harm could come to me. My chill came from my deficiency to comprehend who or what was near me. The light was still too glorious to behold.

Then a presence touched me on my shoulder from behind. My eyelids began to flicker and in an instant, my eyes felt comfortable to focus in the glory. I wanted with all my heart to look behind me and see the presence, yet I was afraid. It was not fear of harm which stopped me; it was reverence that the presence was not human. I was a stranger in a heavenly land and if I turned to look, I feared I would faint. Theologically I did not believe this could be possible, but one experience can shake a thousand theories.

I heard soft footsteps behind me walking away and my attention was drawn to my surroundings. Below my feet was thick grass. It was varying shades of rich green, from dark to light, and many had tiny streaks of yellow and red in them. I reached down to touch the grass and it felt soft, reminding me of a fluffy blanket.

I cautiously took a step forward and the grass slowly bounced, comforting my step and it sprung up again, as if it was lifting me forward for the next step. The grass swayed together in unison and as I drew my gaze into the beyond, there were many green hills before me. The slight smell of ginger and honey lingered in the air.

As I scanned the scene ahead something benign flew slowly past my face. I drew back to focus and I saw what can only be described as tiny round pieces of glittering 'confetti' sailing through the sky, as if blown by a breeze. They danced through the air in groups, like a flock of birds in unison and their colours were gold, silver and fiery bronze. Each one was about the size of a pinhead. As the glittering 'confetti' sailed through the air, thousands of other pieces followed and the radiant light around struck each one making them glitter with a golden kiss of light. They sparkled and it seemed like they communicated with light.

Overhead there was a rich blue sky and as it touched the land in the distance, there was orange light breaking through, like a sunset, with no sun. I saw in the distance flowers unlike any I had ever seen. I walked into their midst and touched them. Some were shaped like golden crowns; they were rich yellow, blue, purple, red and other colours which I could not identify. I touched one and it felt like silk. Then, I noticed they swayed when I touched them, and they released a quiet sound, like that of a triangle being perfectly and gently tapped.

I continued walking up a hill where the flowers resided in numerous numbers and there was no strain on my legs as the elevation grew. As I moved my feet they touched the heads of the flowers, leading them to move into each other. I was aware that none were being trampled under my feet and as they swayed each one released their own distinct musical sound.

There were other sounds around me and I listened carefully. I closed my eyes and quietly dancing on the circle of the sky, I heard the singing of a thousand choirs in unison.

The first choir I heard was similar to the sound of Europeans singing in a cathedral, such as on a royal occasion. Then, I distinctly heard Asian and African choirs singing songs of worship. It was honest and true, and I fell to my knees, as my emotions exploded with adoration and praise to God. In this intensified state, I also discerned songs of praise that I recognised from the Pacific.

On earth, I thought of these expressions of worship as being uniquely separate from each other; here they blended as one, in perfect pitch as if orchestrated by a master. I sensed that every form of worship on earth was a small sample of the pendulum swing of God's expressive nature, which He planted in the hearts and cultures of mankind. Here they are united in perfect harmony.

There was also a deeper level to the worship that I heard; it was an angelic sound that underpinned all, encompassing the forms of praise, whilst catching their essence and corresponding.

I was aware I was in a timeless place, however, I still chose to measure time by the standards of earth. Perhaps time could be described in simplistic terms as the continuum of experience in which events pass from the past, through the present and to the future; but what happens when there is no past or future? What happens when you step out of time? Eternity is the absence of time.

By earthly standards, this tiny foray into eternity had lasted longer than twelve hours and there was no approach of night, for there was no sun on the horizon to set (Revelation 22:5). I felt no fatigue and no desire to lie down, to rest or sleep.

My whole being had been drawn deeply into the worship I heard and it was innocently mesmerising. I felt lost in the praise of eternity and was swept off my feet, and my spirit within was floating. God inhabited the praises of His people in an invisible mist of intensity (Psalm 22:3), and His presence was heavy upon my being, and light on the soul. On earth, I had worshipped in large crowds and when I chose to forget self, and the musicians ministered quietly in the Spirit, I was able to feel that God was near. Yet here it was thousands of times the intensity. I was drawn into love and love overcame me (Song of Solomon 2:4, Romans 5:5).

The invisible worshippers sang of the holiness of the Lord, and although we had tried to use the same words and phrases on earth, by these standards, every attempt of earthly praise felt tainted and unclean. The worship was in Spirit and in truth (John 4:23-24). I almost felt the desire to apologise for corrupting worship on earth and bringing it down to a human level.

I had read in the Bible that day and night people are lost in praise in heaven, and I did not know how it could be possible; yet when pure love, joy and light floods into you during worship, the thought is not how long will this go on for, but please may it never stop!

I felt like a child in a favourite playground, undesirous and unaware that anything could surpass this moment. Suddenly, the unseen presence touched me on my shoulder again and I was gently eased out of rest, with the knowledge I had a journey ahead.

I walked onwards to the top of a nearby hill to determine what was over the ridge. As my head reached over the peak, I witnessed valleys and hills, all were green and lush. Glorious light filled every part of the land and illuminated every area, bathing it in various colours with the sunlight of His Divine and perfect love. To the far left, there were several thunderous waterfalls and still rivers, with many kinds of plants and flowers growing (Psalm 42:7).

In my spirit a Scripture sprung forth: 'The Lord is My Shepherd, I shall not want. He makes me lie down in green pastures; He leads me beside the still waters, He restores My soul' (Psalm 23:1-3). These words were being literally fulfilled in heaven!

To my great surprise, I saw about thirty small white and pink clouds hovering just five-feet above the ground. One was creeping up the hill in my direction and I stepped back as it flowed slowly forward. I reached out to touch it and it felt soft, solid and light. It also felt strong; I held onto it and its movement forced me to walk with it. I was aware it was ascending and I knew that if I kept holding on it would lift me off the ground! In a spirit of discovery I held on a little too long and my feet lifted slightly into the air. I let go and with a bounce landed on my feet.

The most beautiful locations on earth seemed to be a marred glimpse of this world. I was also aware that I was limited in my ability to describe what was before me. How can you describe a world which has no comparison? There are things and experiences in heaven which are unspeakable (2 Corinthians 12:4); perhaps language itself is too limited. How can you explain an experience that overcomes the soul and spirit to such an extent that you are driven to silent peace and holy ecstasy? How can you share an encounter which feels too sacred for words?

I had appreciated the greatest natural wonders of earth

primarily by sight, but here, the way I felt was just as important. I was filled with a sense of wonder and imagination. This heavenly revelation had finally been received with something charming and glorious wherever I turned. The feelings that overtook me reminded me of an excited child on Christmas morning and I was surprised I could still feel such things. The childlike sense of wonder, delight and imagination, which are stolen from us by the harsh realities of life, came flooding back.

Then there was joy. Oh, what joy! It was like discovering I had missed out on some new wonderful feeling which existed all along. I felt joy inexpressible and full of glory (1 Peter 1:8). It was flowing into me, pressed down and flooding over (Luke 6:38). Yet, I must also confess that my hypocritical pious religious attitude made me subdue this experience, because even though feeling joy is God's will, my religious heritage made me question it.

I felt within myself the urge to resist this counterfeit 'pious' religious attitude of melancholy, that takes captive so many Christians, with the exhortation, "Do not sorrow, for the joy of the Lord is your strength" (Nehemiah 8:10).

Chapter Two

Three Visitors

Standing on top of the hill I watched as the heavenly land opened before me; I cannot explain how – somehow it literally revealed itself. The landscape breathed like a sunflower on earth, which opens and follows the sun, and whilst this occurred, I felt a strange sense I had been here before. I knew I had not visited in a physical sense, however many things felt familiar. I had prayed for months to see heaven – did I visit in a dream and to protect me from pride only my subconscious was found faithful to recall such events?

I gazed into the distance to the tops of the hills and valleys, and figures were standing still. There were angels stood in a row, silently watching. They were tall, dressed in white and stood astride like warriors. Their presence brought reassurance.

Suddenly, out of the gleaming hazy light nearby walked two small figures. It was two little angels bathed in white light, wingless, and to my amazement, they appeared like children aged five or six.

I wondered why they appeared in such a form and then I sensed a thought placed into my consciousness. Their appearance was arranged specifically to reassure me. Nothing was threatening about them. The angels in the distance were good, but they also looked ready for war; meanwhile, these angels projected childlike charm, trust and simplicity. They appeared like a boy and a girl to reassure me, but this was not their true form (Hebrews 13:2).

The angels came close to me reaching out their hands and holding a beige book. It appeared to be hundreds of years old. The edges of the cover were worn and the sides had turned light brown; it must have come from earth. I slowly took hold of it and a pulse came from it like a slight electric current which spoke saying, "Truth."

The angels looked me in the eye and there was such gentleness within them, as they communicated with me without using words.

"This is the guide to your journey," they said. "Read what you see and see what you read."

I trembled as the book opened of its own accord and rested in 2

Corinthians 12. I knew this was the Book of books! Then the 'girl' angel, as she appeared, slowly raised her hand and pointed her tiny finger to two verses which I read in my heart.

"I know a man in Christ who fourteen years ago – whether in the body I do not know, or whether out of the body I do not know, God knows – such a one was caught up to the third heaven. He was caught up into paradise and heard inexpressible words, which it is not lawful for a man to utter" (2 Corinthians 12:2, 4).

The angels communicated again with me in my heart. I cannot recall the exact phrases they used, as they explained that my experience in heaven would be limited by my humanity. The carnal mind of Adam (inherited by all humans) has become so distorted that I was partially blinded (Psalm 51:5, Romans 5:14). I had to be cautious and I was warned I must not misinterpret all I witnessed.

The pages of the Book began to feel warm again and one of the angels pointed again to some verses. I read them silently.

"But we impart a secret and hidden wisdom of God, which God decreed before the ages for our glory. As it is written: 'No eye has seen, nor ear heard, nor the heart of man imagined, what God has prepared for those who love Him.' But God has revealed them to us through His Spirit' " (1 Corinthians 2:7-10).

What struck me about this passage was the concept that our imaginations are limited and no person has seen, heard or dreamed of all God has prepared for His people. I imagined the Creator designing mankind, then designing a world in which every sense was overwhelmed! I saw His handiwork planting desires into many hearts and then in heaven, those desires were fulfilled extravagantly. Nevertheless, God has given us a glimpse of heaven through visions and revelations which agree with Scripture.

"Do you understand what Paul wrote?" asked a deep and powerful voice from behind.

I jumped at the voice and turned around to encounter a seven-foot tall angel. I stepped back and tripped as I moved my feet quickly. I fell backwards and as my body touched the grass it enveloped me and bounced as if it was expecting to catch me. The two childlike angels giggled with fun and spoke to my heart. "He's friendly," they said. "He is stern, but he is good."

The angel was strong and powerful. He radiated with glittering light and wore a pure white robe. He had no wings and I was not told his name. As I thought about his appearance, the girl angel spoke to me in my heart.

"You see him in a form that comforts you," she said, "not as he is."

The two angels whispered in each other's ear, giggled and lifted their hands to wave goodbye. I hoped they would stay with me as the large angel was powerful to behold. I waved to them in return and they frantically waved in fun childlike intensity.

Immediately the large angel stood up straight, hands on his hips, waiting for a response to his question which I had almost forgotten.

"What did Paul write?" I said hesitantly, realising that this was the first time I had spoken out loud in heaven. "He wrote that no human has seen, heard or imagined what God has prepared," I said in haste, "but God has revealed them through His Spirit."

"Where is the chronicle of their revelations?" asked the angel.

"In the Bible," I replied, "in the books of Revelation, Thessalonians, in the Gospels and so forth."

"Have you studied what God revealed to them?" the angel asked.

"Not enough," I said, feeling a little embarrassed.

"Don't you want to know about your future home?" he asked with care. "Why is it you know the plots of fictional stories and can quote from them, whilst you remain ignorant of your eternal home?"

I sought an excuse to justify myself, but found subterfuge is not welcome in heaven.

"Is the Spirit of the Lord restricted?" He asked in a whisper, as he challenged me (Micah 2:7). "Do you embrace the stories of the world more than the story of God? Do you love the world and the things of the world? (1 John 2:15). Why do you not know what happens when you die? Paul wrote: 'To be absent from the body is to be present with the Lord!' This is your hope and yet you remain ignorant of the basics!" (2 Corinthians 5:8).

"Please come back childlike angels and rescue me," I thought. "You were so very easy to be with." As I thought these things the large angel leaned back in laughter. He had read my mind and his laughter comforted me.

"When you are challenged by God or by His representatives," he said, "do not defend yourself or seek justification, humble yourself. This is a law of the Kingdom" (Matthew 23:12, 1 Peter 5:6).

"Please forgive me," I responded. "I am willing to learn in humility."

"Many want to know what heaven will be like," he said, "and you must allow the revelation of the prophets and the apostles to be your guide and measuring line..."

I interrupted him by asking, "Will I see what they saw?"

"You will see what you need to see and you will understand as you are able," he replied. "You see through a glass darkly. You know in part and prophesy in part" (1 Corinthians 13:12).

"Does that mean I can be mistaken?"

"You are quick to ask questions and slow to listen," he warned. "Be careful how you see, for your heart is like the blind man partially healed at Bethsaida, who saw men walking as trees" (Mark 8:24).

"A partial revelation," I uttered.

"Make sure you see the right part," he concluded (Matthew 13:13). "Now I will give you another warning: For many years you have been feeding on the milk of the Word which was designed for newborn babies; now you must begin to eat meat (1 Peter 2:2). At first, it will be hard for you to digest. Yet if you are to grow in faith you must accept solid food and not just the dessert" (1 Corinthians 3:2-3).

Chapter Three

A Golden Cottage

The angel began walking to the north and I stood still wondering what to do. Did he want me to go with him? He continued to walk forward with his back to me and he said, "You will see reflections of what was, is, and is to be."

With those words, I began to follow him at speed to catch up, as he walked over another hill. I was beside him when he raised his arm and pointed. In the distance there was a cottage with at least eight visible windows, the roof was thatched and the walls were golden in colour. Twenty feet in front of the home was a river, gently flowing and it provided a peaceful atmosphere. Around the back, there was a huge waterfall, comparable to Victoria Falls in Africa (Psalm 42:7).

The strange thing about this home was the fact that I knew it reflected the personality of its owner. I had not met him, yet this was a part of his eternal inheritance, which is incorruptible and undefiled. I sensed within my spirit this home had literally been reserved for the owner, an eternal possession which does not fade away, reserved in heaven (1 Peter 1:4). I was reminded of the words of Jesus who said, "I go and prepare a place for you" (John 14:3).

"Is heaven like this for everyone?" I asked the angel.

"What nationality are you?" he inquired.

"I'm British."

"Tell me about Britain."

"I live in England," I told him, "and we sing of a green and pleasant land; it has become part of our national psyche. But the reality is most people live in cities and built-up areas, and we still long for the green and pleasant land."

"What you see here tells me much about you," he concluded.

"Does that mean heaven looks and feels different for each person, depending on their background?"

The angel did not answer my question and pointed towards the house. A man was working in the garden and he was the first non-angelic person I saw. I knew in my spirit he was a miner on earth and I felt very pleased for him, that he had been given such a wonderful mansion.

The angel listened to my thoughts again and gave his

conclusion, "What injustice denied him on earth, he has now been given."

The man waved and began to walk towards me. He was five feet eight tall, with blond hair and was muscular. His body was spiritual in nature (Luke 20:35-36), and I knew he was still without the full glorified body because the end of all things has not taken place (1 Corinthians 15:42-44, 2 Corinthians 5:8, Philippians 3:21).

Nonetheless, he had the vigour of youth and I understood the wisdom of his years by the glory resting upon him (1 Peter 4:14). He was wise in his life, therefore the glory of wisdom shines from him for eternity. I was given insight and in heaven, I believe, people are distinguished not by their old human age, but by the glory upon them (Daniel 12:3). This is a part of God's reward for faithfulness and no-one desires another's glory – all are thankful for their own.

The man from the garden came close to me and I reached out my right hand to shake his.

"Do you still do that down there?" he asked with a smile, as he pushed my hand aside and hugged me. "Up here we truly are one body in Christ. There is no need for distant formality."

"Thank you for meeting me," I replied. "What is your name? Where exactly am I? Oh, I have many questions."

The man smiled as I asked more questions, and with a quiet and humble tone, he said, "First I have a question for you. Will all you ask proceed from faith or doubt?" (Matthew 14:31).

I did not know how to respond to this and he smiled again saying, "This is paradise. It is where those who were troubled find rest. They rest from their labours and their works follow them (1 Thessalonians 3:1). My works followed me – they are the souls which were saved by my confession and labour, and the sacrifices I made for the King and His Kingdom" (2 Thessalonians 1:17, Revelation 14:13).

"I didn't know you were a full-time evangelist," I blurted.

"I was not," he replied. "I was a miner and I had very little on earth, and yet, all I owned belonged to the Lord and the Holy Spirit used it all for the glorification of Jesus (John 13-15, John 16:7). I suffered much in life, for it was very hard; yet I now consider those sufferings are not worthy to be compared with the glory revealed in me (Romans 8:18). The words of Christ have now been fulfilled in my life: 'Blessed are you poor, for yours is the Kingdom of God. Blessed are you who hunger now, for you shall be filled. Blessed are you who weep now, for you shall laugh' " (Luke 6:20-21).

"How much of your time on earth do you recall?" I asked.

"I can remember certain events," he replied. "Looking back at my life is similar to dwelling on the years of one's childhood. As a child, the months appeared to pass very slowly and I wondered if I would ever become a man. Then I grew up and my faraway childhood years began to take on a dreamlike quality. As an adult, I could still recall events, happy times and sadness. Nevertheless, the emotions of those years are gone. Eternity has sealed them. It's like a dream."

"You know your life on earth was real and presently it all feels like a dream," I replied. "That's intriguing."

"Have you ever dreamed the perfect dream and woke up to a disappointing reality?" he asked. "Here we live the dream and the disappointments of our former lives are forgotten in the glory.

"It is no accident that the angel brought you to me. My ministry is to help people like you who visit heaven. I've seen many people over my time and to each I show similar things and something new. To each, I appear in a different form."

"Your job is to help people who visit heaven," I stated. "Do you get tired of your work?"

"I will answer this question and then I must testify of all you need to know," he replied.

"No-one gets tired of their work in heaven because all serve the Lord doing work which He created them to love. This was God's original plan for earth. Adam enjoyed his role in naming the animals. However, when Adam and Eve sinned, a curse came upon the earth and all work came under the curse. Survival and work became hard and toilsome because of sin (Genesis 3:16-19, 24). Due to this, Adam and Eve were expelled from the paradise of Eden. To survive the harsh sinful world they created by their rebellion, they would shed much sweat, blood and tears; and the process of childbirth would be painful. They never returned to their paradise.

"Unfortunately for all mankind, their sin did not affect them alone, because every human descendant would bear this punishment. All would have to toil and struggle in a fallen world, dominated by the god of this world, who works to blind people to the truth and make their lives a misery through sin (2 Corinthians 4:4).

"Oh, praise be to God – that curse has no power here and we live in the freedom God originally intended. In this eternal home, people work for their heavenly Father serving Him in jobs they love to do, and their ministry fulfils the dreams God placed within their hearts from a young age. All the misery and toil of earthly work is past, and calling what we do here as work is a misnomer. We love what we do, and look forward to all we do and shall do."

"That sound's wonderful!"

"Now, I need to tell you about my first experiences in heaven. I will start from the beginning," he said with joy. "When I first arrived in paradise, I visited an area far from here, with tall trees, comparable to the giant redwood trees of California. Everything around me was perfect. The colours were more vibrant, the smells authentic and the joy within – how can I describe it – praise be to God! I had never seen anything like it before. The very best of earth seemed to be like a reflection of a beautiful garden seen in muddy water. Suddenly I could see it all clearly in perfect light. Have you ever seen a picture of the most ideal location and wished you could visit? Now imagine it becoming so overshadowed by something better that it now appears to be ugly. That was my experience. Everything I had seen and known does not compare."

"You inspire me," I said. "You explain heaven far better than I."

"Paradise was and continues to be truly wonderful," he continued. "Nevertheless, it wasn't the splendour which overwhelmed me – rather it was the fact I was pain-free at last! For years in life, I had suffered from my joints because of decades working down the mines. I had pain in every part of my body at times; it was hard to read, difficult to walk…it was difficult to do anything. Sometimes I prayed for just one day free of pain. Can you imagine waking up to pain every day and feeling it throughout the night? As the years passed and I became elderly it became almost impossible to walk up the stairs because my natural energy and vigour were exhausted. I had to stop and catch my breath just to take one step.

"Can you imagine, therefore how I felt on my very first day here? I commenced my new life by praising God for my spiritual body because I was pain-free! Then I ran, and ran, and ran, excited that the zeal of youth was mine for eternity (Psalm 103:5, Isaiah 40:31). Every sickness, every ailment was gone and I was pain-free. I was young again. I never realised I would experience the zeal of youth anew and it was magnified beyond all I had known before. One of my favourite Scriptures became very real to me:

" 'Those who wait on the Lord shall renew their strength. They shall mount up with wings like eagles. They shall run and not be weary. They shall walk and not faint' (Isaiah 40:31).

"It took me weeks, earth time, to adjust to my new reality without running everywhere. In my mind, I recalled my last moments on earth, lying on my deathbed in pain, thinking my life would soon be over. Then I was in paradise and I realised this was the beginning of my real life (Luke 23:43, 2 Corinthians 5:6). My existence before was an introduction to this fullness. The first page of the first chapter of my life was written on earth, now new pages and new chapters are added, and each chapter is better than the one before.

"As heaven changed my view of everything, I became aware of something which never truly gripped me on earth – I was created as an eternal spirit. I am a spirit (Romans 1:9, 8:16, 1 Corinthians 2:11), which possesses a soul (Matthew 16:26), who happened to live in a body whilst on earth (Romans 6:12). I don't know exactly how to explain this to you, as you are...well...still carnal."

"You speak the truth," I confessed. "Please go on."

"I was now living in the environment God designed me for. I was finally in my element; this is home. In my old life I was like a cyclist on a racing bike bogged down in the mud – all seemed to be an endless effort. Then in heaven, it was like discovering asphalt for the first time. I was like a fish trapped in a muddy ditch of water believing this was all there was and then I found the sea of eternity! Once I feared death even though I believed in heaven. But now I realise this is what life is intended to be – the old life was similar to a cheap blurred black and white photocopy – this is full colour in high definition. I hope you understand these analogies?

"Something very special also happened to my character and nature. In my life, I became a Christian, yet my nature was still carnal (Romans 7:14), and my mind needed to be continually renewed (Romans 1:2). I was like the apostle Paul who did the things he did not want to do and did not do what he wanted (Romans 7:15-25). Then when I entered paradise something changed within me and I was conformed to the image of Christ. I did not want to sin and I could not sin. The carnal nature was gone and I saw myself in a different heavenly light (Galatians 6:15).

"As the Bible foretold: 'But you have come to Mount Zion and the city of the living God...to the general assembly and Church of the firstborn who are registered in heaven, to God the Judge of all, to the spirits of just men made perfect' (Hebrews 12:23). I became one of the spirits of just men made perfect! (John 3:5, James 2:26).

"On earth, the nature of Adam had distorted my true self because I was and had always been created in the image of God (Genesis 1:27). With Adam's curse fully broken (Psalm 51:5), I bore the image of the second Adam in truth and all the grubby fingerprints of sinful desire were removed (1 Corinthians 15:47).

In my life I had to 'put on the new man who is renewed in knowledge according to the image of Him who created him' (Colossians 3:10); now the new man was put on me! Christ changed me on the inside, as the nature He planted within me fully expressed itself! When I trusted in Christ I became a new creature by faith and I had to fight to allow the 'new man' to express itself as the old was crucified (Luke 9:23). Now the new creature in Christ expressed itself from within as my only nature, because I was released from the flesh (2 Corinthians 5:17).

"As all this change overcame me in paradise, my friends and family were weeping by my empty body (2 Corinthians 5:6-8). If I could have, I would have shouted to them, 'Don't weep for me; weep for the loss you feel. I am more alive now than ever. I am healed, whole and young. I am free, delivered and transformed in Christ!'

"In my lifetime, I did not allow myself to fully explore the truth that the soul and spirit are eternal. You must remember when people die it is only their bodies that are buried – their true self goes on to heaven or hell. It's a change of address, not an end of existence.

"On earth, you mourn for those who are no longer with you and this is needful because death is the enemy of God. Nevertheless, in Christ, death has been defeated (1 Corinthians 15:26, Revelation 20:14). Mourning is good, yet don't allow yourself to forget that those who trusted in Christ continue to live in a better world which is far more real than the life you know.

"People were sad when Moses and Elijah were taken to heaven, yet when the Lord Jesus Christ was on the Mount of Transfiguration Peter witnessed they were still very much alive (Mark 9:5). Even Jesus told the people of His day that Abraham, Isaac and Jacob are still living. For 'He is not the God of the dead, but the living, for all live to Him' (Luke 20:37-38). It is the same with everyone who leaves your world in Christ."

He then told me some personal testimonies to help me.

"People's experiences in heaven are different, so I can only tell you my own. After I celebrated my youthfulness, I then met the members of my family and friends who trusted in Christ, and the ones who helped me find Him. How can I describe those meetings!

"I talked to my father again. Oh, the joy. I told him many things which I always wanted to say to him. We laughed together and I got to know him in a way which was not possible before."

Pausing for a second he continued saying, "I should explain this to you. When I first arrived the past was very much alive. However, after I was completely healed, emotionally purged and restored in a wonderful display of God's power, my old life faded further away, becoming like a dream. Even the old bonds between people became different and much better. It's not easy for me to describe to you; it's something akin to the time when you first become an adult and your relationship with other adults change. They do not treat you as a child and you don't feel like a child.

"I spent some time meeting many people who passed into this life before me – notice I did not say, people who died, for they are alive. It was such a wonderful reunion with all. I won't indulge your time with my personal experiences; you get the idea.

"After this, I met the Lord Jesus and the Father! Well, I could speak to you about that encounter for weeks and never fully explain how wonderful it was. Let me say this simple thing – imagine floating in a river of love and glory. You will understand more of this later and will discover why I was asked to hold my tongue on this matter.

"What I can tell you is that my old doubts about God now seemed ridiculous in His majesty (Psalm 14:1). If I could have, I would have felt embarrassed at the possibility that I once entertained such foolish doubts about His power or goodness (Hebrews 11:6). I found myself confessing, 'In Your presence is the fullness of joy; at your right hand are pleasures forevermore' (Psalm 16:11)

"Then I suddenly understood how He had guided my life all along as I obeyed Him. He had been blessing me, assisting me and He used difficult life lessons to teach me (James 1:4). I found myself acknowledging, 'It was You all along!' You must know what I mean? I'm speaking about the unseen and holy presence in the room; or the feeling that events in life have been altered by a power greater than all we can understand…and so forth. I realised I had been quick to complain when things went wrong; whilst being ignorant of all the secret and hidden things God did for me.

"I never considered that He was constantly intervening in my life to change things for the better. Imagine an angel coming to you and asking, 'Did you thank God for saving your life today – by stopping the car crash?' In your ignorance, you would have replied, 'I didn't have a car crash today,' and the angel declares, 'Exactly!'

"As I dwell on this I wondered how many times I announced,

'That was close,' or 'I'm glad that worked out,' or 'what a coincidence' etc. Now I know it was God working in the unseen realm, answering prayer, caring for me and proving His faithfulness by miracles unseen. He didn't tell me what He was doing because He expected me to live by faith, not by sight (2 Corinthians 5:7).

"I also found there is another side to this story. I discovered how my disobedience to the Lord and the teaching in the Bible greatly hindered His plans, will and blessings. I learnt how my sin gave the enemy power to harass me and some of the things that happened to me were my fault; I reaped what I sowed into other people's lives (Galatians 6:7-8). My eyes were opened to learn how I missed out on much by stepping out of His perfect will; by doing so I left the road of blessing. Yet He forgave me! Praise Him!

"After I discovered this I was shown to my mansion and was given time to travel around heaven, to meet people and explore. Many of my rewards for my obedience were given to me and there is still more to come after the Lord ends all things. One of the great blessings God gave me is a home by this wonderful waterfall. Can you imagine seeing this every day? On earth all I mostly saw were bricks from my windows – now I have a majestic view.

"There is no time here," he explained. "The simplest way I can describe it, is for you to imagine a clock which never counts forwards or backwards; it's a timeless reality without day or night. We never weary and do not need to rest or sleep. For me, every moment feels like the first day of a holiday, which you have looked forward to for years. It's a constant thrill.

"After I settled and became familiar with my new home, I was given this job of meeting visitors and helping people. I guide them around and tell them what they need to know. In this way, each visitor brings more news from eternity about life in heaven. Some misreport, misunderstand or interpret things slightly different than they should have – so be careful and check all with the Bible – yet the message of preparing for heaven continues to be spread."

His words inspired me and I acknowledged, "You have given me a perspective which I have never seen before."

"There is more to be seen," he replied. "The heaven which you now see is the first stage in God's eternal plan for His people. After the return of Christ to earth, the millennial reign will commence, followed by a new heaven and earth, where believers will rule and reign with Christ. There is much more to be revealed to you about this at another time" (Isaiah 11:6-9, Ezekiel 36:27-30, Matthew 25:31-36, 2 Timothy 2:12, Revelation 5:10, 20:1-6, 21:1, 22:5).

"I could talk to you for hours asking questions and receiving revelations," I expressed. "It's all too wonderful to describe."

"We will talk much," he replied. "Nonetheless, all you have heard so far is the 'dessert' of eternity, and there are some heavy 'meat and vegetables' to come (1 Corinthians 3:2, Hebrews 5:12). So you must have ears to hear and be careful not to try to understand all. Faith doesn't need to ask 'why' about everything. There is only one question in heaven which overcomes us and saturates our thinking. It was the question Jesus asked on the cross, as His humanity compelled Him to ask a question, whose answer He already knew. His question was so profound that your Bible has it written in two languages – 'Eloi, Eloi, lama sabachthani?' which is translated, 'My God, My God, why have You forsaken Me?' (Mark 15:34).

"These are the words the thief on the cross heard," he continued, "and you are now where the thief was rewarded for his penitent heart and faith in Jesus Christ (Luke 23:43). We still find it hard to comprehend why the Lord chose to suffer so bitterly for us all. You tend to focus on His physical suffering; in heaven, we dwell on the cost of separation from the Father and the costly humility of the incarnation. As the hymn of Charles Wesley states: 'God contracted to a span. Incomprehensibly made man. He laid His glory by. He wrapped Him in our clay.'

I was encouraged by the testimony of this heavenly man and asked him, "Please tell me your name. You have said so much and I still do not know your name."

"You love names on earth and many who are called by Christ want their names to be well-known," he warned, "the pride of man is no secret. Yet there is a great victory in remaining anonymous to give Him all the glory (Judges 13:18). Accountability means this is not always possible, but for me it is; so I choose to deny my name and glorify His."

Chapter Four

The Gate of Heaven

The angel had been silently listening to our conversation when he reached out his hand and touched my shoulder, and we moved from the valley to the gate of heaven (Psalm 118:19-20, Luke 13:24). The way we travelled was new. We did not walk, nor were we lifted and moved in the spirit. Imagine the fabric of paradise was an elastic band; normally you would walk from one end to the other; yet if it was crumpled together, you could walk vast distances in one step. This is what took place, as the fabric of paradise was both crumpled together and stretched at the same time. In this context, we can choose to walk the long route or travel quickly.

The Bible in my hand began to feel very hot again and I opened it, and a passage was highlighted by a glow of light. I read it to myself, "Surely goodness and mercy shall follow me all the days of my life and I will dwell in the house of the Lord forever" (Psalm 23:6).

"There remains therefore, a rest for the people of God," said the angel, and he pointed towards the narrow gate of heaven (Matthew 7:14, Hebrews 4:9). On the back of the gate which is on the inside of paradise, there was a quote from the Bible. 'Precious in the sight of the Lord is the death of His saints' (Psalm 116:15).

Another verse appeared in rotation and it testified of the tragedy and eternal hope of people who die before they have lived a full life:

'The righteous perishes and no man takes it to heart. Merciful men are taken away, while no one considers that the righteous is taken away from evil. He shall enter peace' (Isaiah 57:1-2).

I gazed upon the gate of heaven and watched as people walked into paradise. Those who entered were greeted by people who went before them into heaven, especially those who had been saved by their testimony (Luke 16:23, Revelation 14:13). They all received new heavenly bodies and their faces were different, yet they were still recognisable. It reminded me of seeing a childhood friend whom you haven't seen since he or she was a child. Even though an adult now stands before you, it is often still possible to 'see' the person you once knew.

A wave of joy overtook me as I saw reunions taking place. Heaven once seemed like a far-off land; now I knew it is our true home. We have always been heading towards eternity and death represents not the end of life; but rather a period of temporal separation. The process of life then death will continue on earth, but the desire for heaven has always been within us because God has placed eternity in our hearts (Ecclesiastes 3:11).

Those who entered into paradise were perfect in every way. Every person looked different and each one reflected the glory of God in a fresh way (2 Corinthians 3:18). They were ageless, blameless and whole. If I had to describe their spiritual presence I would say once again, they had the vigour of youth (Isaiah 40:31).

I stood by as a godly woman walked through the gate and was transformed before me. Though I refer to her using a female pronoun such as 'she,' I saw her transform into a spiritual being, neither female, nor male (Matthew 22:30, Hebrews 1:7, 13-14).

Before she went through the gate she was the spiritual presence of her former self on earth, and in the process of walking through she metamorphosed into a new heavenly likeness. I recognised her with spiritual discernment, yet she was different. It reminded me of the resurrected Jesus on the road to Emmaus as He walked with two disciples in a different form (Luke 24:15-16, 32).

I cannot represent accurately or precisely what happened and I was reminded of the words of John. 'Beloved, now we are children of God and it has not yet been revealed what we shall be, but we know that when He is revealed, we shall be like Him, for we shall see Him as He is' (1 John 3:2).

Suddenly something caught my attention out of the corner of my eye. I turned to see the letters of an unknown alphabet flying through the air. They moved too quickly for me to count and I was unable to recognise them from anything before. They flew rapidly towards the gate, and the woman who had just been transformed opened her mouth and they entered her.

"She is now fluent in the pure heavenly language," said the man (Genesis 11:1, Zephaniah 3:9).

Now, you must understand, I did not percieve any men or women here, as all are spiritual beings like the angels (Luke 20:35). However, as I cannot speak the heavenly language, I still have to use earthly terminology to describe them. I still use the terms 'man' or 'woman' as they help me to clarify descriptions, but my language remains limited by my humanity.

"Come with me," the man insisted, "and I will show you the

other side of the gate."

The angel placed one of his hands on my shoulder and the other on the man who spoke. Science as we know it does not apply in heaven and explaining the details of how I moved here is not easy. Nevertheless, the 'space' which we occupied was 'stretched' and 'contracted' and we travelled with it to the entrance of the gate.

"I love this job," expressed the man with joy, "we all say that."

"Does everyone work in heaven?" I asked.

"There's no unemployment here," he said with a smile in a light-hearted manner. "You didn't believe we all floated around on the clouds playing harps?" he joked, with other pure jokes following.

I was stunned into silence by the delivery and substance of his comments. Sometimes the reverent religious aspect of people's personalities can make them appear stern and distant, yet this was certainly not the case with this man. I had no idea we were allowed to laugh in heaven. I thought I had to be very serious indeed!

Responding to my hesitation he asked, "Don't you remember Sarah? She doubted God and when Isaac was born she said, 'God has made me laugh and all who hear will laugh with me' (Genesis 21:6). Do you not recall that Jesus said, 'You shall laugh,' when He spoke of heaven? (Luke 6:21). Heaven is the essence of joy. Let me explain, your carnal and distorted religious worldview has been keeping you back from experiencing God's joy. Let it go and allow yourself to laugh, and enjoy being a child of God" (Galatians 4:7).

Suddenly joy hit me and a great 'belly' laugh came from within, and a smile erupted on my face. My austere religious pride resisted and I had to choose to let go of my miserable religious manner, to allow this joy to overcome me. I laughed pure laughter and felt such overwhelming floods of real joy. I was so overcome that I lay down awash with joy. That smile stayed with me for a long time.

After some time, now with a deep inner smile, my eyes were drawn to the area leading towards the entrance to the gate of paradise. There was a cliff edge leading down to earth, and I witnessed people shooting up from the earth, like shooting stars and landing near to the entrance. Falling beside them, as they travelled were sparks of light and the people stopped gently before the gate of paradise.

On the outside of the gate which leads into the wondrous land was inscribed these words to greet all arrivals.

"God will wipe away every tear from their eyes; there shall be no more death, nor sorrow, nor crying. There shall be no more pain, for the former things have passed away" (Revelation 21:4).

Arousing my curiosity this quote also faded and another appeared:

"This is eternal life, that they may know You, the only true God and Jesus Christ whom you have sent" (John 17:3).

"Why does it change?" I asked the man.

"Heaven and earth will pass away, but the words of Christ shall never," he prophesied (Luke 21:33).

I turned to face the crowd of people walking towards the entrance and there was no hurry and no queuing; it all flowed perfectly.

"Who are these people?" I inquired.

"These are the sons and daughters of the resurrection," he stated. "They cannot die anymore, for they are equal to the angels, being the children of God" (Luke 20:36).

Opening a scroll he began to read to the people as they entered through the gate. I heard the promises found in the book of Isaiah.

"He will swallow up death forever," he read confidently. "The Sovereign Lord will wipe away the tears from all faces; He will remove the disgrace of His people" (Isaiah 25:8). Then several people cried out in unison, "Surely this is our God; we trusted in Him and He saved us. This is the Lord and we trusted in Him; let us rejoice and be glad in His salvation" (Isaiah 25:9).

The crowd passed through the gate and the transformation that I had witnessed with the woman was taking place for all, as they were changed from glory to glory (2 Corinthians 3:18).

A new group arrived at the gate and some of them were carrying heavy bags. There was a man, like the one who talked with me and his job was to greet the new arrivals, to help them. He went over to one who was carrying much baggage and took the load from him. I overheard him saying, "Why did you carry these burdens with you all your life? Christ paid the price to set you free (John 8:32, 36). You could have been delivered years ago."

The names on some of these bags were easy to read: rejection, self-hate, weariness, loss, grief, stress, broken-hearted and many others. Some simply stated: 'Bad memories of 1964,' and there were many other years. The man who was helping went over to a woman, took her bags and said, "These are spiritual chains around your heart, which you have carried too long. Let me take them from you in His name" (Philippians 3:13).

Those who walked through the gate were transformed

outwardly, but my focus changed, and I discerned that a further and greater transformation took place – it was the inward change of the soul and spirit! The ugliness of the carnal nature was returned to the purity of Eden (Genesis 3:5, Romans 6:5). This process had begun on earth (Titus 3:5) and could not be completed due to corruption.

The inhabitants of heaven were still waiting for their final heavenly bodies, yet in spirit and soul, they bore the image of Christ.

'It is sown a natural body, it is raised a spiritual body. There is a natural body and there is a spiritual body...As we have borne the image of the man of dust (Adam), we will also bear the image of the heavenly Man (Christ)' (1 Corinthians 15:44, 49).

The people were being changed by the glory, though they still had to wait for the final glorification when death would be swallowed up in victory (1 Corinthians 15:54-56).

I believe this was another part of the fulfilment of the promise that was revealed to Peter. 'By which have been given to us exceeding great and precious promises, that through these you may be partakers of the Divine nature, having escaped the corruption that is in the world through lust' (2 Peter 1:4).

Peter taught we all have our part to play – to choose to let God shape us into His image (2 Peter 1:5-8), yet the final metamorphosis of the inner man takes place when God removes the old nature from us, allowing the 'seeded' nature of Christ to fully reside in fulfilment of Ezekiel's 'new heart and spirit' prophecy (Ezekiel 11:19, 36:26).

On earth, when someone believes in Christ Jesus as Lord, their spirit is born again (John 3:3-7), but their soul (commonly known as the mind, will and emotions) still needs to be renewed (Romans 12:1-2). Paul gave himself entirely to the Lord, yet he struggled with the carnal nature and it was this battle, I believe, that was being won (Romans 7:14-23). Paul had once complained: 'O wretched man that I am! Who will deliver me from this body of death? I thank God – through Jesus Christ our Lord!' (Romans 7:24-25). Therefore with joy, he wrote: 'For whom He foreknew, He also predestined to be conformed to the image of His Son' (Romans 8:29).

When I first encountered people entering paradise I focused on the physical change, as they had no ailments, all were perfect in health. But now I understood that the change inside is far greater. The selfish nature 'seeded' into all the descendants of Adam is fully replaced with the nature of the second Adam (1 Corinthians 15:22). Its akin to a spiritual genetic condition which afflicts all, causing deformities of the soul and spirit, and drives the body to death.

The fruit of Adam was utterly replaced with the fruit of the Spirit! I was reminded, 'The flesh lusts against the Spirit and the Spirit against the flesh...but the fruit of the Spirit is love, joy, peace, longsuffering, kindness, goodness, faithfulness, gentleness and self-control' (Galatians 5:17, 22-23). This is the new nature!

At once it dawned on me that the old selfish human nature could never be allowed in heaven, for it would lead to people mistreating each other. This is one of the reasons, I learnt, why it is impossible for 'everyone to go to heaven.' In heaven do we want to live near Hitler, a thief, an unrepentant adulterer or a troublesome neighbour who mistreats all, including his family?

Only those who welcome God's final stage of the transformation of becoming a 'new creation' in Christ can live in complete harmony with others (John 3:18, 2 Corinthians 5:17, Galatians 6:15).

God's heavenly Kingdom is set on a holy mountain (Revelation 21:10) and in heaven, many of the prophecies of Christ's millennial reign find partial fulfilment, as believers wait for earth's redemption (Romans 8:19-23, Revelation 20:6). In heaven, God takes away the sinful nature within us and delivers us from sinners who refused His Lordship. Besides, those who live holy on earth are grieved by the sin of the world, like Lot was (2 Peter 2:7); we also grieve over our sins. Yet, in heaven, we will not remember our past sins, and we will reside with others who are holy and humble.

"In that day you shall not be ashamed for any of your deeds in which you transgressed against Me," says the Lord. "For then, I will take away from your midst those who rejoice in pride and you shall no longer be haughty in My holy mountain. I will leave in your midst a meek and humble people and they shall trust in the name of the Lord. The remnant of Israel shall do no unrighteousness and speak no lies, nor shall a deceitful tongue be found in their mouth" (Zephaniah 3:11-13).

The strength of the light that shone in heaven was glorious indeed and it comforted my soul. The consistency of the warmth, light and glory provides a constant reminder that I was in perfection. I took personal pleasure in thinking there would be no cold dark winters in heaven. There are no Siberian winters here!

I was also struck that this is a devil free zone. There were many angels and no demons present. I believe Satan has a right to enter the court of heaven (Job 1:6, 2:1, Daniel 7:26, Zechariah 3:6-14), but this is paradise and no demon can harass anyone here.

Nonetheless, some pitifully weak devils tried to test God and enter as they hitchhiked on people's backs. These demons had spiritual bodies with arms and legs. They were skinny to the bone, two-feet in height and their faces were contorted by hatred. They weighed nothing physically, but the spiritual burden of carrying them had been considerable.

When the burdened soul crossed inside paradise these demons were struck with fire, as if a powerful electric current hit them. They had tried to hold onto the carnal nature, trying to grip to the soul of those whose spirit had been redeemed. But they were expelled, and fled in fear and on fire!

I was shocked these weak devils had harassed these souls for so long and the angel hearing my thoughts gave me his conclusion: "The Lord gave His people power over all the works of the enemy – to cast out, bind and expel. But His people are destroyed by lack of knowledge and some foolishly declared a ceasefire on the enemy, despite the fact he never observes any armistice (Hosea 4:6, Luke 9:1, 10:19).

"You are either redeeming the land in your life and nation, or the Kingdom of darkness is plundering, and trying to extend its rule. The Great Commission deals thoroughly with this war between God and Satan's host. You are called not only to share the gospel with every creature, but also to cast out demons, heal the sick and speak with new tongues (Mark 16:15-18). These are the signs of the Kingdom, and if Christians refuse to exercise their authority over the enemy, he will indulge their indifference and ignorance" (Hosea 4:6, Matthew 28:18).

Chapter Five

A Great Reunion

"May I ask," I said to the angel with hesitation, as I changed the subject, "why don't you have any wings?"

"I speak to you about the war between the Kingdom of God and Satan," the angel stressed with puzzlement in his expression, "and you stop me, to ask a question which has no relevance to your journey. You ask, not to learn – rather to boast to others that you know... Now I will answer your pride with a question. Do you believe the paintings you have seen of angels on earth are authentic?"

Western imagery of angels may include wings, like the Seraphim's (Isaiah 6:2), but how can heavenly beings be drawn authentically? I could not answer the angel and thankfully he pointed to the man, indicating I should follow him over another hill and into a new valley. I began to slowly jog to get towards the man and I was not feeling tired. The grass beneath my feet was wonderful and I recalled that Jesus taught that God designed it (Luke 12:28).

When I caught up with the man at the top of the hill, I viewed the valley below and there was a great multitude without number. There were people from every tribe, tongue, people and nation (Revelation 5:9). I was amazed I could recognise the nations which some of the people came from. Like John, I too witnessed various tribes and tongues. On earth nationality and ethnicity has often been a tool for separating people, yet in heaven everyone is equal, and there is no greatness or shame attached to the former (Galatians 3:28). All are God's family and citizens of heaven (Philippians 3:20-21).

I wondered how long the various nationalities would be distinct in heaven. Would I always be 'formally' British or would my new identity as a citizen of heaven evolve within me, so that one day the former would not be remembered? Perhaps I had to wait for the new heaven and earth before that took place (Isaiah 65:17).

My eyes were then drawn to the east, as I witnessed a grown woman being directed by one of the angels to find her mother. I discovered that many reunions were taking place in this valley. When they met, they threw their arms around each other and wept.

I wanted to know their story and asked, "What happened to them?"

"The mother died of cancer when the daughter was only six," the man explained. "The daughter always felt that something was missing in her life because there was a person absent as she grew up. She felt that loss in every major and minor event of her life."

I was thrilled watching these two people being reunited and beheld a spiritual rainbow appearing overhead, coming down and touching them. It was as if God was speaking to them personally stating that the suffering of the past was now over forever (Genesis 9:13-17, 2 Thessalonians 1:7, Revelation 4:3, 10:1).

This experience also drew some questions from my heart.

"I thought there were no tears in heaven?" I insisted.

"Would you deny tears of joy to those who are reunited?" he said.

"It's a question about the Bible," I said.

"No, you have a question about your interpretation of the Bible," he replied. "The Bible promises that God will wipe away every tear (Revelation 21:4), and as that woman has just entered paradise she has a season of personal adjustment, to experience healing from the past in preparation for the fullness of God's glory to be revealed in her. Those two are like women who knew great pain in childbirth and now the pain will be forgotten in their joy" (John 16:21-22).

"I don't understand."

"Samuel was at rest, but he still recalled the troubles of earth (1 Samuel 28:3,15-25). Have you not considered Lazarus?"

Jesus told a parable about Lazarus who lay at the gate of a rich man's home, hoping to eat his leftover crumbs (Luke 16:19-31). Lazarus had been a victim on earth and now he was comforted in paradise. The rich man however, was sent to hell. As I thought about these two people I realised that both could recall their experiences on earth. For Lazarus, the happiness of his new life more than compensated for his suffering on earth. He was healed in heaven and was free from the past; whilst the rich man was tormented in hell because of his former selfishness.

In heaven, the suffering of earth will one day be forgotten, yet the martyrs of heaven had a recollection of the past for a season, in order for them to witness justice taking place. Meanwhile, in that transitional phase, they were rewarded for waiting for God's final judgment on those who had taken their lives (Revelation 6:10-11).

As I considered this, I found my imperfect conclusions. When we first enter paradise perhaps we are given the opportunity to find closure from the past. Maybe we have the chance to say the things we neglected or were unable to say. We can meet those whom we loved, but never saw and be reunited with those we lost. It is a place of total rest, reunion, reconciliation and final closure.

I opened the Bible and read a verse that never grows old. "He will wipe away every tear from their eyes and death shall be no more, neither shall there be mourning, nor crying, nor pain anymore, for the former things have passed away" (Revelation 21:4).

"Do you see the progression?" asked the man. "God will wipe away every tear from their eyes; before He can wipe away those tears people must be given the opportunity to release them. Then, when their hearts are purged there will be no more crying or mourning."

"Why is it necessary to experience such things?" I asked.

"Healing does not take place when your memory is erased," he said, "but when your soul and spirit is purged, healed and restored to newness. Those who have lost a loved one do not want to forget, they want to meet again and experience the joy of reunion.

"There are many people who have buried pain in their heart and it has overshadowed their lives. Some put hurt out of reach because of their family responsibilities, others because they felt unwilling or unable to confront the pain. The focus in heaven is never on pain or the former suffering, but on the release and healing.

"Nevertheless, for those whose suffering was cruel, they may choose to receive total healing instantly without any remembrance. Whatever people choose, in the fullness of His time all the former things shall pass away and will be forgotten" (Isaiah 65:17).

We had talked the theory and then I laid my eyes on a former military man searching for his family. On earth, he had fought for others in a righteous battle and he died in a foreign land. His wife and children never truly recovered from the loss. Life went on for them and outwardly they all smiled on cue. Yet, whilst others forgot his and their sacrifice, this family had a constant ache in their heart and a hidden backdrop of emotional deprivation that clouded all. The years changed, but in some ways, they all lived frozen in time to the date they learnt of his death. Life for them was divided into two parts: before and after they heard.

Suddenly, I saw him walking through the fields towards his family and they ran towards him and embraced. I could not hear what they said to one another because it was a private concern; I believed they spoke of all the lost years. It was a beautiful reunion and I stood in awe, as I felt unseen streams of healing waters flowing towards them, wiping away their tears and replacing their pain with the fullness of God's absolute healing. The years the locust had eaten were restored in a moment (Joel 2:25).

This was not the only reunion that inspired me, for I came across people from every walk of life being reunited. I saw families who were separated by natural death, victims of accidents, natural disasters and various diseases, all meeting with those they loved, friends and family; every pain in the soul and spirit were healed.

The restoration was so glorious that it seemed that the loss of the past resulted in the increasing of the joy of those involved (Romans 5:20). I listened as many spoke about the glory of paradise and the joy of being healed from tragedy. The hope before me was so precious that I sat down and watched the healing streams of God's love flow into the lives of all. Hallelujah for restoration!

Chapter Six

Millions of Angels

I silently dwelt on these events when my attention was drawn to the enticing sound of laughter over the next hill.

"May I look over there?" I asked the angel.

"Not everyone can accept what they see over that hill," he replied. "The light of the truth can be harsh for those who have lived in the dark."

"I wish to be a child of the light," I announced, as the angel pointed to the hill and I accepted this as a sign of approval.

"You must understand something," said the man as he came with us. "God does not desire to hurt people, nor make them feel guilty for all they have confessed. There is no condemnation for those who are in Christ, who walk according to the Spirit" (Romans 8:1).

"I know that," I uttered impetuously, "let's go on."

"No, you do not know," said the angel, as his face brimmed with compassion. "When people have sat in the dark, it can hurt them to see the brightness of His light. Truth can be blunt and some find it easier to be blind, rather than view the penetrating light of reality."

I felt concerned about what I would see over the hill. I knew it would be serious and I had to be prepared to allow the truth to penetrate my heart. Therefore, I reached forward and placed my hand on the man's shoulder and he led the way. With the assurance he was guiding me, I closed my eyes and took each step cautiously. Still unable to see by choice, my mind focused on what I heard and I tuned in intently. It was the sound of millions of voices, laughing, playing and having fun. It was a beautiful sound.

"Open your eyes," said the angel, "and see the truth."

I obeyed and before me was a vision I had never experienced before. The millions of voices came from children. They were running, smiling, laughing and enjoying life abundantly (John 10:10). Some bounced against the clouds that floated above the ground; others were jumping off the hills and the soft grass was catching them like a trampoline. Some were picking flowers; others were blowing the tiny pieces of glittering 'confetti' which floated through the air and chased them. I saw angels with them dancing and acting out stories from the Bible. I was so thrilled by the fun of it all and felt surprised I had been concerned about this revelation.

"Who are these children?" I asked the man.

"These are the innocents," said the angel, as he chose to answer my question, "those who were lost, those who were taken and those who were rejected."

Suddenly a chill went down my spine. Whenever the angel spoke to me it always felt serious; and the man added to his words speaking more softly than ever before, trying to avoid any attention.

"He speaks of miscarriages, children who were victims of disease, natural disasters, crime and abor..."

As he tried to finish his words the angel placed his hand over the man's mouth, and the children turned on mass towards us, with one finger placed over their lips indicating silence. From above a voice testified, "It is not the will of your Father in heaven that one of these little ones should perish" (Matthew 18:10, 14), and I shook in holy fear. In that exact moment, I was given further insight into the history of some of the children before me. Some were victims of crime and many children had been killed in acts of genocide, notably from Africa. There were multitudes from Western nations, China and India. Asian girls far outnumbered the boys because males are often preferred in Asia.

"Every child is sacred to God," the angel said, as he considered the numbers of children who had returned to play in celebration. "They were all formed by the miracle of God in their mothers' wombs (Psalm 139:13-16). He watched from on High as they grew into His image and was tender to each, and their spirit returned to God who gave them (Ecclesiastes 12:7). So where sin abounded on earth, grace abounded much more in heaven" (Romans 5:20).

Amongst all the children, I saw one mother who had recently arrived in paradise. When she came through the gate she had met many family members and she chose to have this encounter on her own. She was searching for her child and an angel had been sent with her as a guide. Then, from the midst of the crowd, there was a young girl, around six years old, with pigtails and pink ribbons in her hair running towards her. The mother opened her arms and burst into tears of joy as the child fell into her embrace. They had never met before and somehow by the gift of God they knew each other.

"Mummy!" the girl cried out with a long drawn-out sound.

For a long time, they both seemed unable to say anything else, for to hug was enough. Later the child whispered in her mother's ear the name God had given to her. The mother seemed overwhelmed by this revelation, and she lost all the strength in her legs and fell vertically straight down, into a crossed-legged position.

"This is the name I gave you," said the mother, "and I never got to call you by it."

"No, mummy," said the child, "this is the name that God gave to you on earth and to me in heaven. It was a special bond between us that you never knew."

In a seated position I observed for what seemed like an hour earth time. The child lay in her mother's arms and they talked about life on earth and in heaven. The child explained in heaven she had never been without a father.

"God is a Father of the fatherless," she told her (Psalm 68:5).

This reunion was one of the most special encounters I felt in paradise. It seemed to me in heaven, God exercises His role as Father in a very personal way. This is His holy habitation where there is no suffering (Revelation 21:4), and due to this, it is the perfect place to be a child.

Amongst the children were many angels who had the responsibility to look after them, to play with them and to encourage. I wondered how God was able to spare so many angels for these roles; then I recalled Jesus' teaching.

"Take heed that you do not despise one of these little ones, for I say to you that in heaven their angels always see the face of My Father who is in heaven" (Matthew 18:10).

Originally these angels were assigned to plead to God for children on earth, but in heaven, they were reassigned to care for them. The angels gave the children assistance all the time, and each child had a very personal relationship with God the Father and the Lord Jesus Christ; they were close to each one.

"Jesus loved children," the man stressed. "Christ said, 'Let the little children come to Me and do not forbid them, for of such is the Kingdom of God' (Luke 18:16). Paradise is now their home. Here the fatherless are finally defended" (Psalm 82:3).

"God is their Father," I cried out. "What a wonderful sight."

"This is true," said the angel, "and there is more," he stressed. "On earth, some men choose to forget they are fathers, some even deny the child in the womb; but in eternity, they will see the truth and they will feel the full weight of their sin (Malachi 2:14-17). They must repent whilst they have time, and there is no repentance without a drastic change in behaviour and attitude.

To the women who have been abandoned I tell you this, 'God has seen their struggle.' Too often, the full weight of the burden of the consequences of the sin of what is called 'the sexual liberalisation of society' is born by women. In their millions they have been used, abused, hurt and abandoned. God has seen their struggles. Many have stood in the gap and it is a righteous cause to fight for a child to have a better life."

"There are others who feel guilty," added the man. "Sometimes we hear the prayers of people who feel shame over their past. But they have forgotten that everything that is confessed to God is cleansed by the blood of Jesus and there is no more remembrance of it. You can search all of heaven and there is no record of any confessed sin. He promised, 'Their sins and their lawless deeds I will remember no more' (Hebrews 10:17). He makes a choice to forgive and He chooses to forget. Therefore every child of God must also forgive self and be released from the burden of his or her past. As God has forgiven him or her, the individual must follow God's lead and stop chastising self, to receive His grace-filled forgiveness."

As we talked, a powerful wind blew in the distance and I saw it creeping over the grass towards us. I watched it slowly moving through the landscape and the glittering 'confetti' which blew through the air was caught in its vacuum.

"What is happening?" I asked.

The angel pointed towards the woman with her child. The speed of the wind was picking up, and it hit the woman and child. The tears in her eyes were swept away by its power and a painful cloud within her was dragged out, as the healing waters flowed in.

"God is wiping away her tears," the man told me.

The strength of the wind was so strong that it crept towards me and hit me with great power, and blew into every part of my being. As soon as it touched me it felt as liquid love.

"You are feeling a little of what she feels," said the angel.

The strength of this power was so great that it touched me deep in the inner man. I tried to restrain my emotions, but every part of me exploded in release. Plumbing the depths of my soul, this love poured through memories of the past and many were uncovered as hidden pain was granted liberty (Isaiah 61:1-3).

I struggled to understand what was happening, as it felt like an intensified version of the release one feels from the deepest tears one has ever cried, yet there was no pain associated with it. As the love of God flooded into the hidden recesses of my soul, any grief was overcome with Christ's love. It was like darkness fleeing from the light. In an instant, it was gone and I was left with a sense of victory. I was aware that inner restoration had taken place. It was the evacuation of pain, and I chose to rest and abide in Him as this peace flooded my being. I must have been there for hours and later when I felt able to speak, I asked to experience it all again!

"Who will enter this paradise and experience this joy?" I asked.

"He who does the will of God," the man replied.

"What is His will?"

"This is His will," he said, "that everyone shall believe on Christ Jesus the Lord and have everlasting life (John 6:40). Therefore, do not be like the Pharisees who rejected the will of God, as they refused to humble themselves and repent" (Luke 7:30).

"How can I be sure this is God's will?" I asked.

"John described the will of God – 'and this is His commandment that we should believe on the name of His Son Jesus Christ and love one another, as He gave us commandment' " (1 John 3:23).

"All I must do is simply believe," I announced.

"There's more to it than making a vague declaration of faith," he replied. "Peter preached you must repent and be baptised in the name of Jesus Christ for the remission of your sins, and then you can receive the gift of the Holy Spirit (Acts 2:38). If you confess with your mouth the Lord Jesus and believe in your heart that God has raised Him from the dead – and if you truly believe you will be saved because your life will change forever!" (Romans 10:8-9, Acts 16:31).

"Faith in Christ is the door to paradise," I concluded (John 10:9).

"There is more to heaven than paradise," he stressed. "There is heaven and the 'heaven of heavens' (Nehemiah 9:6). You have seen a little. Paul saw the third heaven and what you see now is temporal. There will be a new heaven and new earth, yet many of the first saints have been serving in heaven for almost two thousand years. There is much to do and this heaven lasts long!"

"How does time work between the heavens," I asked. "How does earth time and heaven work? How can people from earth, limited by time, become reunited with others that abide in the unlimited realm of eternity?"

The angel did not acknowledge my question and I pondered the timelessness of heaven. We experience life in the arrangement of past, present and future; yet as this realm is beyond time, I expect that events on earth can change dramatically (years and decades can pass, and it all may feel very long ago); meanwhile in heaven, maybe it feels like only a month or a second has passed (2 Peter 3:8). Perhaps when children go to heaven their childhood is prolonged, or maybe the parent's earthly timeline and that of the child's cross. Perhaps the entire concept of time itself is a hindrance and each generation steps into eternity at a similar point. With no firm conclusion outside of the timelessness of God, I comforted myself with the knowledge we will meet again, with those who trusted in Christ (Joel 2:25, Colossians 1:15).

King David experienced a family tragedy and looked forward to a reunion in heaven. His son was sick and he prayed, fasted and wept hoping for a miracle. Then after the child died, David chose to walk with God and receive His strength for the future. He worshipped the Lord concluding: 'He is dead...can I bring him back again? I shall go to him, but he shall not return to me. Then David comforted his wife' (2 Samuel 12:23-24).

I had made many mistakes on this journey and as I focused on these things I was probably trying to 'understand' everything, instead of believing by faith God has all under control. Faith is substance!

Chapter Seven

The Heavenly Body

The angel guided me back to the entrance of the gate to paradise and my attention was drawn to a crowd of angels gathered. One angel stood about a foot taller than the others. A song of celebration was being played and people began to gather.

"What is happening?" I asked.

"Someone important is entering," he replied.

I strolled towards a space on high ground about thirty meters away. The new arrival stepped through the gate towards the crowd. There was a great celebration with shouts of joy and hugs. It resembled watching the greeting of a family of close and loving people.

As the new arrival walked through the crowd I found it impossible to see the physical appearance of this person's previous existence. I could not discern if this person had been male or female. The glory that rested was so great that it appeared as a physical cloud of light bursting forth from the inside of the person's heavenly body.

"Excuse me," I said to a passer-by, "do you know who this person is and what he or she did on earth to gain such an entrance?"

"In her previous life," he expressed, "she was a single Christian woman who devoted her life to Christ. She refused to marry outside of God's will and carried a great sadness in her heart. Her parents died when she was young and because of this she never knew what it felt to be loved, cherished and cared for in a family. She was often alone. Even church 'family services' made her feel excluded. In her life, she had many stories of events that happened to her and feelings which were never expressed to another."

Heaven understood this woman's pain and I was beginning to learn that the wrongs of life are put right in eternity. Those who were once forgotten are now openly celebrated (Luke 6:21).

"The Father also reserves these great welcomes for the poor, the broken-hearted and the lonely," the passer-by told me. "He comforts all who grieved and gives them beauty for ashes, the oil of joy for mourning, and the garment of praise for the spirit of heaviness. They are now called trees of righteousness, the planting of the Lord" (Isaiah 61:1-3).

In the distance, I noticed on the other side of the gate, a strange sight. There was a thick warm mist covering it and through the glory I saw a woman, still bent over, walking towards the gate (Luke 13:11-17). Through the crowd, I sought the man who walked with me and he was not present. I was silent for a short while, but I had to inquire, so I turned to the angel asking, "Why is that woman still bent over? She should be completely whole!"

"She is whole," replied the angel, "but her sickness became such a part of her on earth, that she still thinks like a sick person" (John 5:6, Romans 12:1-2, Ephesians 4:23, Colossians 3:10).

With this, the bent-over woman walked through the gate and I heard a Divine voice like thunder crying out, "Come forth!" (John 11:43). Suddenly beams of light hit her body and she stood up straight, being completely released from the bondage in her mind, which she had brought with her from earth.

These experiences brought me great joy and they also raised several questions. What kind of body will we receive in heaven? Why couldn't I recognise the gender of the woman? Do we still have personal relationships in heaven and so forth?

Paul visited the third heaven and he did not know if he still had his physical body with him (1 Corinthians 12:2-3). However, it was revealed to him that there are several types of bodies.

'There are also celestial bodies and terrestrial bodies,' he wrote: 'but the glory of the celestial is one and the glory of the terrestrial is another' (1 Corinthians 15:40).

Sheepishly I asked the angel, "Can you help me find the answers to my questions about our bodies?"

"What did Christ teach?" was his reply.

When the angel said this to me my first thought was this – if the man was here, he would have given me a straight answer, instead of answering me with a question. However, as the angel could read my thoughts and knew my heart (Hebrews 4:12), I quickly changed my thoughts, and tried to answer the question!

Perhaps the angel was trying to reveal to me that too often I expected preachers to spoon-feed me the Word of God and answer my questions. Instead of getting close to God myself in prayer and studying Scripture; and rather than read books by Bible teachers to understand the truth, I had been too passive.

"What did Christ teach about our existence in heaven?" I thought.

I was drawn to the time Jesus talked about the resurrection and I remembered He gave clear instructions concerning eternity. In the Gospel of Matthew Jesus taught:

"For in the resurrection they neither marry, nor are given in marriage, but are like angels of God in heaven" (Matthew 22:30).

The phrase they "are like angels of God in heaven," reoccurred in my mind. What are the angels of God like? What do they do and how similar shall we be to them? Fortunately, the Bible is full of references to angels.

Angels do not have physical bodies of flesh and blood, but are spirits (Psalm 104:4, Hebrews 1:7, 2:16). God also is Spirit (John 4:24). When Christ was raised from the dead, He encouraged His disciples that He was not in His spiritual body by stating, "Behold My hands and My feet, that it is I. Handle Me and see, for a spirit does not have flesh and bones as you see I have" (Luke 24:39).

Then I considered one of the primary Scriptures that describe angels. 'Are they not all ministering spirits sent forth to minister for those who will inherit salvation?' (Hebrews 1:14).

When a human being dies that person's body is left behind on earth and it decays; whilst the spirit departs into the new world of the heavenly realm. The Psalmist describes this process. 'His spirit departs; he (his body) returns to the ground' (Psalm 146:4).

Humans are restricted by their physical bodies of flesh and bone, but the heavenly body given to them by God will be free of many of these limitations. Jesus said we would be like the angels and the only way I could explore what He meant, was to learn more about angels. How do they serve God?

When Abraham went to sacrifice his son Isaac, an angel stopped him (Genesis 22:11). Angels also went on a mission (Genesis 19:1). Angels serve God and are aware of events on earth (Genesis 28:12, 1 Corinthians 4:9). They have been called upon to help many of the most important leaders in the plan of God (Genesis 32:1), and some are warriors (Matthew 26:53). Angels are sent on protective missions because they are strong and powerful (Psalm 91:11, 103:20). Also, when they visit earth some have the ability to blend into the crowd and look like humans (Hebrews 13:2).

In heaven, angels speak directly to the Father on behalf of children (Matthew 18:10) and they enjoy worshipping God (Psalm 148:2). Angels do not marry (Matthew 22:30) and they do not know all of God's plans (1 Peter 1:12).

In the life of Christ, angels were sent to announce His birth (Luke 2:9-14) and they ministered to Him in times of testing (Matthew 4:11). Angels may eat and when they visit earth in human form they have eaten with men (1 Kings 19:5-8).

However, when the Scripture details 'angels' food,' it may be poetical because Christ is the Bread of Heaven (Psalm 78:24-25), and Jesus' food was to do the will of His Father (John 4:31-34). On earth, food is a fuel for mankind to give energy and it produces waste. It seems that these two will not be necessary in heaven for spiritual beings. As there is nothing harmful that can enter the body in heaven, nothing harmful needs to be flushed out, expelled, or filtered. There is no waste.

Angels have their own language and some humans have spoken their language in the Spirit (1 Corinthians 13:1). Angels have emotions and experience joy when sinners repent (Luke 15:10). They are also assigned to churches (Revelation 1:20), and they carried Lazarus to Abraham's bosom when he died (Luke 16:22). They will also be reapers at the end of the age (Matthew 13:39-49, 24:31); and will return with Christ (Matthew 16:27, 2 Thessalonians 1:7). At the time of judgment, they will witness Christ confessing the names of His people (Luke 12:8, Revelation 3:5).

Angels currently have a higher standing than humans (Psalm 8:5, Hebrews 2:7) and they have free will; some choose to disobey God (Job 4:18, Hebrews 2:2, 2 Peter 2:4,11, Jude 1:6).

In the next life, redeemed and transformed believers shall be promoted to the role of judging angels (1 Corinthians 6:3); thus there is a day of judgment for them too.

It is sinful to worship angels and to give them undue regard (Colossians 2:18, Revelation 22:8-9) because they must worship Christ (Hebrews 1:6), whom they are subject to (1 Peter 3:22). In the meanwhile, some will have important roles in the end times (Revelation 7:1-2, 11, 8:13-15), including war (Revelation 12:7-9).

There is much in the Bible about angels, including a tantalising passage which is interpreted by some theologians as a reference to a human who was promoted to an angelic role: 'The angel who showed me these things... said, "For I am your fellow servant and of your brethren the prophets, and of those who keep the words of this book. Worship God" ' (Revelation 22:8-9).

"The Bible tells us so much about angels," I told the angel. "But which parts of their lives will apply to humans in our eternal home?"

"You ask many questions," he replied, "faith must be your answer."

As I pondered the Scriptures, I concluded that believers may well have three bodies in their lives. The first is the human or natural body as Paul calls it, which is sown in corruption in death, unless Christ returns (Romans 8:23, 1 Corinthians 15:44, 1 Thessalonians 4:15-17). The second is the spiritual pre-resurrection body, which John witnessed when he saw the multitudes of saints in heaven. This is the spiritual body we inhabit as we wait for the resurrection and transformation of our physical bodies from earth (1 Corinthians 15:42-43). Paul described this state, 'To be absent from the body and to be present with the Lord' (2 Corinthians 4:6). The final body we will possess is the resurrected body, which will be united with our heavenly body – combining all three into one (1 Corinthians 15:52). In this sense all three bodies are one, waiting for unification!

As with all my conclusions, I have to submit them acknowledging we do not see the full picture and there will be more to learn. But we do have this promise, that our 'Saviour, the Lord Jesus Christ, will transform our lowly bodies that it may be conformed to His glorious body' (Philippians 3:20-21).

Chapter Eight

A Change in our Nature

The words of Christ concerning our new status in heaven provides answers and it also raises questions (Luke 20:34-36). The concept of being reunited with friends and family in heaven and meeting heroes of the faith is comforting (Hebrews 12:1). People with happy marriages may seek a reunion; yet what about unhappy ones?

On earth, the reasons for marriage are recorded in the Bible. The first is to provide companionship so people are not alone. Another is to provide both parties with a helpmate and there is a sexual bond which renders a pure union for godly procreation (Malachi 2:15), and physical intimacy (Genesis 2:18, 1 Corinthians 7:5).

However, Jesus taught, "In the resurrection they neither marry nor are given in marriage, but are like angels." Therefore, He explained that life will be profoundly different in heaven (Matthew 22:30). In eternity, we will not need to have one special bond with one person because our nature will be changed. The religious rules of marriage will no longer apply and no one will desire marriage anymore. The sexes and the marriage covenant will cease (1 Corinthians 7:39).

Jesus addressed this question because the Sadducees asked Him about a woman who had been married seven times by saying, "Whose wife shall she become?" (Luke 20:27-33). The Sadducees did not believe in the resurrection, and the first reason Jesus gave for there being no heavenly marriages was to acknowledge that human beings may have several spouses in a lifetime and these bonds do not extend into eternity.

In paradise, we discover the fullness of what it means to be spiritually married to the Lord (Romans 7:4, 2 Corinthians 11:2), and we become fully aware of what it means to be part of His very large family; we will all be related by His blood. This means there will be no exclusion because all are one in Christ (Galatians 3:28).

Some couples have been fortunate to experience an unbreakable bond of love. However when Christ is revealed to them and in them, perhaps they will become so in love with Him, that the human bond of the past will not matter any more.

Romantic love between the sexes was beautiful in its time; yet in heaven, we become like the angels with heavenly bodies and we find true eternal love in Christ Jesus our Lord (1 Peter 1:8).

When love is experienced on earth it serves to be a blurred reflection of Christ's love for His Church (Ephesians 4:24, 32). It could even be suggested that the greatest experiences of sacrificial romantic love between a man and a woman is a shadow of Christ's love for His people. Perhaps those moments of abandonment to romantic love provide us with an insight into God's endless love for the world. It is passionate, overwhelming and insightfully 'blind' to the cost. It is blind love by choice, which also fully knows! He knew the cost of the cross and still chose to love us.

Therefore in heaven when we experience His fullness of love, the more we are wrapped up in His love, perhaps the less we will recall the old bonds on earth. The past held precious memories for some, yet the glory of the future makes it pale into insignificance.

As there are no males or females in heaven, we will all enter a period of absolute equality between the former sexes. In that Divine presence, our nature will be changed in such a way, that the way we relate to one another will be fully transformed. We will not need marriage because the former desire will be replaced with Him.

In heaven, we will be "equal to the angels" and "sons of the resurrection" (Luke 20:36); and the longer we stay in His glory, the more God will penetrate our soul and spirit to transform them. We will be changed from glory to glory (2 Corinthians 3:18), and each new glory will make the past fade away. The past was good in its time but when God's perfect plan has come to fruition, there will be no need for the old reflection (Philippians 3:13).

As there is no marriage in heaven, what happens about those who want to see their spouse again? With our finite minds we only see a blurred reflection of the whole (1 Corinthians 13:12); with this in mind, I came to believe that there is an initial transitional period in glory, where husbands and wives may meet in the spirit with the knowledge of the past. Yet the change within us will mean there is no sense of loss for the past, just glory for the future. Then the longer we live in God's presence, the less we think of the old. All of this is part of the preparation for the fulfilment of all things when there will be a new heaven and earth, and 'the former shall not be remembered or come to mind' (Isaiah 65:17). These were only my thoughts based on my interpretation of Scripture, and I had to accept the warning from the angel, that I should not try to understand all. Walking by faith does not mean we understand everything, rather it means trusting completely in God's goodness.

Nevertheless, I should conclude this with something I recall from the great reunions. I saw a husband and his wife who had fought for years over everything. When I witnessed them meeting for the first time in heaven I thought – "Oh no" – but instead of arguing, they laughed at themselves. They joked about their foolishness and conceded how full of pride, self-centred and carnal they had been. They praised God for their new nature and the past was forgotten. Whenever they saw each other again, it was always with a smile.

Chapter Nine

The Heavenly City

"Are you prepared to enter the heavenly city?" the angel asked.
I nodded affirmatively in self-confidence.

"Those who have confidence in themselves will fall short," he cautioned in mercy (Philippians 3:3).

The angel knew me better than I knew myself and exposed many selfish thoughts and desires with such few words. I was a child of earth, walking in the heavenlies and I could not hide my human nature in such purity, and transparency.

In Christian doctrine, we teach that the nature of Adam has infected the human race, and I had forgotten how that doctrine is outworked in me! In the world, many argue that human nature is essentially good; yet we never need any tutoring to be selfish or to hurt others; it comes naturally. If we read modern statistical research or examine history about our failings it is shocking. Almost every week new reports are published exposing terrible injustice, abuse of power and neglect of righteousness. All this sin is the nature of Adam expressing itself through humans (1 Corinthians 15:22).

The Church tends to focus on 'those outside,' but Jesus taught we must look inward and challenge ourselves to live to His standards (Matthew 7:3, 1 Corinthians 3:13). Paul wrote: 'Examine yourselves as to whether you are in the faith. Test yourselves. Do you not know that Jesus Christ is in you? – Unless indeed you are disqualified!' (2 Corinthians 13:5). This continual acknowledgement of the sinful nature should help us to face the truth, yet I found it hard to see myself from heavenly standards.

The angel tapped me on my back with care, to encourage me to walk with him and I was grateful for his gesture of affirmation. We were still walking in the green valleys and were accompanied by the man, who had been so accommodating to me. He answered many of my questions and treated me in such a way, as if he still remembered what it was to be flesh and blood.

Then, in the distance, I caught my first glimpse of the heavenly Jerusalem. There was a narrow road ahead, leading up to a great and high mountain, and on top, the heavenly city resided (Revelation 21:10). The walls were huge, for it was impossible to see to the top and they cast no shadow. The city was square; its length, breadth and height are all the same (Revelation 21:16).

We followed the road to the city and after some time on the route, we were stopped by two angels. There was a conversation between the angel who led me and the angels guarding the route. I did not understand them because they spoke in the heavenly language, yet I believe they were investigating whether or not I had the right to enter the city.

"Why do they need to stop us?" I asked the man.

"They are checking if your name is written in the Lamb's Book of Life," he replied (Exodus 32:33, Daniel 12:1, Philippians 4:3, Revelation 21:27, 22:19). "Do you not recall the Master's teaching? There was a man who wanted to enter into the Lord's presence without wearing the proper garment of faith and he was cast out (Matthew 22:11-14). The desire to enter is not enough; you must wear the garment of faith in Christ."

The angels smiled and beckoned me to continue as we followed the path upwards. Then suddenly I heard a voice in my spirit that caused me to shiver and to search to see who was speaking.

"Enter through the narrow gate," the voice whispered. "For wide is the gate and broad is the road that leads to destruction, and many enter through it. But small is the gate and narrow the road that leads to life and only a few find it" (Matthew 7:13-15).

"Are you ok?" asked the man. "You look very pale."

"Someone spoke to me," I confirmed.

"He does that," he said. "This is His city. Heed what He said and look at all before you."

I obeyed as we walked closer to the city wall. The glory of God was radiating bright light. It looked equal to tens of thousands of enormous searchlights, shining up into the sky and shooting out over the city. The light was not just white; it was similar to the colours of precious stones, clear as crystal and radiant. The city was pure gold, yet not like the gold I had known. Here gold is similar to clear glass in its purest form. The walls were jasper in colour and splendid to behold, and its foundations were adorned with all kinds of precious stones: the first was jasper, the second sapphire, the third chalcedony and the fourth emerald. There were twelve gates, each had a large angel stationed in place and the gate itself was one solid pearl (Revelation 21:11-21).

"This is what John saw," the man told me. "The new Jerusalem, waiting in heaven ready to come down from God, prepared as a bride adorned for her husband" (Hebrews 12:22, Revelation 21:2).

There was so much to experience that I forgot myself and fired off several questions without thinking. "Why is the city as high, as it is wide? Why is it so tall? Why does the city need so much space in the air? Does this speak of protection from the outside, or are there homes in what I would call the sky? Can we fly in heaven? Are we free from gravity?" I imagined myself flying to a house in the sky!

"Why do you lack faith?" asked the angel with honest penetrating eyes. "God has revealed all you need to know in the Bible."

I followed my two guides through the solid pearl gate. Inside the city, I witnessed a brilliant white light, too overwhelming to focus upon, like the sun on its brightest day, plus a thousand times the magnitude. I had to close my eyes because of the glory and I recalled what the light felt like. It reminded me of the hottest day of the year in England, when the heat of the sun penetrated my being and brought strength and warmth. I felt the joy of the Lord from the glory and it is our strength (Nehemiah 8:10). The sunshine of God's glory was bringing life to my soul and spirit.

The angel touched my shoulder, and I was able to open my eyes and focus in the glory. I was inside the city whose builder and maker is God (Hebrews 11:10). This is the home of the saints – the eternal heavenly city which all the men and women of faith had hoped for and sought to reside in (Hebrews 13:14).

The first thing that blurted out of my mouth was, "It's bigger on the inside than on the outside!" Just as time is different here, so is space. The city's dimensions hide the enormous space within.

To fully appreciate my surroundings, I first chose to gaze at the transparent gold beneath my feet. The streets of heaven are made with pure gold; it was gold with all impurities taken away.

"In heaven, we trample on the riches of the earth," the man informed me. "Gold is common here, it is all around us (Revelation 21:18). In heaven, we value the Redeemer and those He redeemed."

I lifted my eyes to view the buildings all around. I was struck by the sheer size of them. I could only describe them as mansions. There were no tiny buildings, nor any rooms for people forced to share. There was plenty of room for all. I tried and failed to describe to myself how these buildings appeared because they were different from all the homes I had seen before. I found myself thinking: "This is the perfect design. Why didn't anyone think of this before?"

"This is the city the fathers of the faith sought," said the man. The Bible he held then opened to the book of Hebrews and I read from it.

" 'For these died in faith, not having received the promise, but having seen them afar off were assured of them, embraced them and confessed that they were strangers and pilgrims on earth. For those who say such things declare plainly that they seek a homeland; and truly if they had called to mind that country from which they had come out, they would have had the opportunity to return. But now they desire a better, that is a heavenly country. Therefore, God is not ashamed to be called their God, for He has prepared a city for them' (Hebrews 11:13-16).

As I finished reading, a door of one of the mansions opened and a citizen of the heavenly Jerusalem walked onto the golden street. His body was glowing with glory from without and glory within. Many others came out of their mansions too. They lived in peace with one another. I noticed none locked their doors because this is a place of complete safety; there is no crime, for there are no criminals (Ezekiel 28:24-26). I watched someone walk into another's home to leave a precious gift for the owner as a surprise. The selfish nature within them had been removed and Divine love shaped every relationship (1 Corinthians 15:44, 49).

The streets became full of people as they walked with a sense of purpose and destiny. They all appeared to be heading to do important work and all had joy exploding from their eyes. Some greeted those around with glad tidings, as others communicated in their spirit with the Father.

Suddenly, I heard a voice from beside me crying out, "Behold, the tabernacle of God is with men, and He will dwell with them, and they shall be His people. God Himself will be with them and be their God!" (Revelation 21:3).

I turned to see who was crying out and it was the angel who had accompanied me on my journey. I looked at him with astonishment and he looked me directly in the eyes with a smile.

There was great excitement in the city and in my spirit, I felt footsteps – like a giant's which shook the spiritual ground.

"He is on the move," someone cried out. "He is on the move!"

"Who is on the move?" I inquired.

"You know His name," the angel replied. "He is the Lion of the Tribe of Judah, the Bright and Morning Star, the Alpha and the Omega, the First and the Last, the Beginning and the End!"

The people were excited to meet their God again and they shone brightly with powerful glory. The angel knew my thoughts and educated me. "Those who are wise shall shine like the brightness of the firmament and those who turn many to righteousness like the stars forever and ever" (Daniel 12:3,

Philippians 2:15).

"Why are some brighter than others?" I asked with self-assurance.

The angel looked sad; I had become too familiar with him. Nevertheless, what was wrong with my question?

"You are dividing glory from glory," concluded the man. "Humans are divisive and it starts when you are young. You are taught to believe you are better than some and others are better than you. You are taught to dislike people from one side of town or other areas. You are told which nations are your enemies and who are friends. It is not so here."

"Does that mean everyone is equal?"

"We all rejoice in the glory God has given to us," he said. "We do not covet another's glory."

"Why are there different types of glory?"

The man handed me the Bible and I was told without words by another voice to read various passages of Scripture.

"Knowing that from the Lord you will receive the reward of the inheritance, for you serve the Lord Christ" (Colossians 3:24), and, "Look to yourselves, that we do not lose those things we worked for, but that we may receive a full reward (2 John 1:8). For the Son of Man...will reward each according to his works" (Matthew 16:27).

"There are rewards in heaven and rewards during the millennial reign," he said. "The Lord said, 'Assuredly I say to you, that in the regeneration, when the Son of Man sits on the throne of His glory...everyone who has left houses or brothers or sisters or father or mother or wife or children or lands, for My name's sake, shall receive a hundredfold, and inherit eternal life. But many who are first will be last and the last first' (Matthew 19:27-30).

"There are many rewards," the man testified. "Rewards for those who overcome persecution (Matthew 5:12), or temptation (James 1:12), rewards for selfless love (Matthew 5:46), for secret giving (Matthew 6:1-4), for faithfulness (Luke 16:10), for secret prayer (Matthew 6:5-6), for fasting (Matthew 6:16-18), for all forms of goodness and grace (Ephesians 6:8), for financial support to spread the gospel through evangelism and missionary endeavour (John 4:35-37, Philippians 4:17), and rewards for welcoming prophets, children and servants of God!" (Matthew 10:41-42).

"I love rewards," I professed with enthusiasm.

"There are many rewards documented in Scripture," he replied. "Jesus taught there are rewards when people hate you, exclude you, revile you and call you evil for His sake (Luke 6:20-23).

There are also rewards for those who love their enemies and do good to others, lending hoping for nothing in return (Luke 6:35-36). There are other rewards for those who struggle against unrighteousness and stand up for truth, even when it hurts (Luke 21:12-19).

"There are rewards for helping forgotten widows, orphans and the despised, for they are precious to God and the Kingdom of God belongs to such as these (Luke 18:16). Learn from the Bible! There are many examples of faithful widows who served the Lord with sincerity of heart; they were despised by the world and by the religious, yet it was the overlooked women and widows of the Bible who were of great importance to Jesus (Malachi 3:5, Mark 12:40-43, Luke 2:37, Acts 9:41). Remember pure and undefiled religion is to help such as these (James 1:27), and it was, and still is many of these forgotten women who help advance the Kingdom of God by providing endless prayer and support for God's work (Luke 8:3).

"There are rewards for those who plant the seed of the gospel, rewards for those who water the seed and rewards for those who reap" (1 Corinthians 3:6-9). Then he warned me. "You must heed John's words – be careful to 'receive a full reward' " (2 John 1:8).

"No-one labours in vain!" I replied with joy (1 Corinthians 15:58). "God remembers everything we do for Him with a pure heart."

As we spoke of this I saw a woman walking through the city with a glory, unlike any other glory I had witnessed. I turned to the man and asked, "What is her glory?"

"She kept the covenant against all odds," he exclaimed.

"What covenant?"

"She married as a teenager before she was able to discern the character of the man she committed herself to," he explained. "Many times she was encouraged to leave him because he was cold, distant and unbelieving. Yet she knew her covenant was made not just with a man, but before God (Numbers 30:2, Hebrews 13:4, 2 Peter 2:20). She suffered much in silence, as her altar was covered with many tears, weeping and crying (Malachi 2:13-15). She knew that God hates the spiritual violence of divorce and stayed true to her covenant before God (Malachi 2:16, Matthew 19:9). Now in heaven, she is rewarded for her faithfulness to the covenant for God (Luke 6:32-36, 1 Corinthians 7:10-11, Ephesians 5:2), and her reward, and all others who follow in her example will be great (Luke 6:35). She understood that she made a covenant, not just a promise (Proverbs 20:25, Ecclesiastes 5:2-7), and she respected Christ's teaching. Jesus defined marriage as a lifelong covenant relationship between a man and a woman for life (Matthew 19:3-8, Luke 16:18). Therefore Christ honours those who honour Him. This is why this woman and all others who are faithful will share a special glory."

"We don't teach on covenants anymore," I stated. "The emphasis today is more about how one feels."

"Your feelings will forever change," he warned, "and if you follow them you become the servant of a dithering fool. The deepest level of any commitment one can make is a covenant with and before God. Covenants are treated by your generation as empty promises, but this is not so with God. Making a covenant and treating it with contempt is condemned in Scripture. 'Can he break a covenant and still be delivered? Since he despised the oath (before the Lord)...My oath which he despised and My covenant which he broke, I will recompense on his own head' (Ezekiel 17:15, 18-19).

"Marriage reflects the covenant Christ made with His Church and it should not be treated with contempt (Matthew 22:2, Hebrews 6:4-6). It was for this reason, the disciples stated it is good to remain single (Matthew 19:11), rather than make a covenant before God and break it. They knew covenants are sacred to God."

"But many were married without understanding the sacredness of making a covenant," I insisted. "Is there no mercy for them?"

"There will always be grace, mercy and forgiveness available," he confirmed. "God understands the brokenness many feel because God is a divorcee and He knows the suffering of being an innocent party betrayed by an unfaithful spouse" (Hosea 2:2, 19-20).

"I'm sorry!" I interjected. "Did you just say...?"

"God was the innocent party in His marriage to Israel," he replied. "They committed adultery and He issued them with a certificate of divorce (Jeremiah 3:8, 20). Nevertheless, He constantly sought restoration and was always prepared to forgive" (Jeremiah 3:22).

"I never knew God felt the pain of divorce," I replied.

"Why are you ignorant of the Scriptures?" the angel interjected in a whisper, as he opened the Bible and prepared to read a verse. The passage he turned to concerned God's feelings about His spiritual marriage to the people He made a covenant with.

"I was crushed by their adulterous heart," he read with anguish. Then the angel paused. I never knew the angel had such deep feelings as he struggled, "...which has departed from Me and by their eyes they play the harlot after their idols" (Ezekiel 6:9).

I was silenced again. Something powerful takes place when a mighty warrior allows his heart to be broken in the Lord's purposes.

"God understands the suffering of the divorcee," the man added, "and He will reward those who suffered because they were faithful to their covenant and suffered whilst doing good" (1 Peter 3:17).

"There are many, many rewards in heaven," the man continued. "Listen to what the Lord foretold, 'Look, I am coming soon, bringing My reward with Me to repay all people according to their deeds. I am the Alpha and the Omega, the First and the Last, the Beginning and the End' " (Revelation 22:12-13).

"I want rewards in heaven," I declared.

"You are saved by grace," he told me, "but you will be rewarded for what you did with your salvation (Matthew 16:27, 1 Peter 1:17). Will you invest your talents wisely or squander them? Those who are self-seeking are of the world and have not the Spirit of God (Romans 2:8). Those who love Jesus by their deeds, will desire to do His good, pleasing and perfect will as they seek for glory, honour and immortality (Romans 2:7). For you are His workmanship, created in Christ Jesus for good works, which God prepared beforehand that you should walk in them" (Ephesians 2:10).

"Help me to live this life," I cried out in prayer to God.

"There are many promises of glory and many crowns," the man announced. "The Lord promised: 'To him who overcomes, I will give some of the hidden manna and I will give him a white stone, and a new name, written on the stone which no one knows but he who receives it' (Revelation 2:17).

"The crown of life has already been given to many martyrs," he added. "The Lord told them, 'Don't be afraid of what you are about to suffer. The devil will throw some of you into prison to test you...if you remain faithful even when facing death, I will give you the crown of life' (Revelation 2:10). Those who have fought the good fight and finish the race can expect the crown of righteousness (2 Timothy 4:7-8), so don't lose your reward!" (2 John 8, Revelation 3:11).

Abruptly from behind, I heard a great thunderous voice, "Blessed is the glory of the Lord from His place!" (Ezekiel 3:12). I then saw multitudes of angels overhead singing, "Holy, holy, holy is the Lord of hosts; the whole earth is full of His glory!" (Isaiah 6:3).

"You have come to Mount Zion and the city of the living God," said the angel. "To the heavenly Jerusalem, to an innumerable company of angels (Hebrews 12:22). The hour has now come, when true worshipers will worship the Father in spirit and truth. God is Spirit and those who worship Him must worship in spirit and truth" (John 4:23-24).

"Come and worship in truth," the man encouraged.

Then within my spirit, something stirred up and I cried out, "You will show me the path of life. In Your presence is fullness of joy; at Your right hand are pleasures forevermore (Psalm 16:11). As for me, I will see Your face in righteousness, I shall be satisfied when I awake in Your likeness" (Psalm 17:15).

"He is prophesying," I heard someone nearby say.

"Your eyes will see the King in His beauty; they will see the land that is very far off (Isaiah 33:17). You will say to the prisoners, 'Go forth,' and to those who are in darkness 'show yourselves.' They shall neither hunger nor thirst, neither heat nor sun shall strike them; for He who has mercy on them will lead them, even by the springs of water He will guide them' (Isaiah 49:9-10).

"Blessed are the pure in heart," I continued, "for they shall see God (Matthew 5:8). For we know that if our earthly house, this tent, is destroyed, we have a building from God, a house not made with hands, eternal in the heavens" (2 Corinthians 5:1).

I was surprised by my outbursts, as those around stared at me.

"I'm sorry," I said. "It just burst out of me. It was like Jeremiah. It was burning within me; I had to let it flood out!" (Jeremiah 20:9).

"We all experience this," the man assessed. "This is why many worship continuously. It is not tedious; it flows from the joy within. We cry out in praise because we love to praise. In every moment, we witness a new aspect of the glory of God and we cry holy."

Chapter Ten

The First and the Last

There was something unique about worship in heaven; for it truly was in Spirit and the truth of Christ. Those who worshipped put their lives into the Truth and because He is their Lord, they sang with conviction. He was in them and all were in Him. The praise and worship of the heavenly city was pure joy.

I also heard many voices singing in a vivid celebration. It was a unique sound which shook and reverberated around heaven.

"What is this noise?" I asked the man.

"Someone just received their citizenship," he replied.

"What citizenship?"

"Of heaven," he declared (Luke 10:20, Philippians 3:20-21). "The Lord said, 'I say to you there will be more joy in heaven over one sinner who repents than over ninety-nine just persons who need no repentance...Likewise, I say to you, there is joy in the presence of the angels of God over one sinner who repents' " (Luke 15:7, 10).

"I've read that many times," I said, "yet I've never really thought of it taking place literally."

"If this new citizen of the Kingdom sets his mind on things above, he will get a greater prize," the man added.

I wondered to myself what this meant.

"Don't you realise that in a race everyone runs?" he said, discerning my puzzlement, "but only one person gets the prize. So run to win! All athletes are disciplined in their training. They sacrifice to win a prize which will fade away, but you do it for an eternal prize! So you should run with purpose in every step. You are not just shadowboxing. You should discipline your body like an athlete, training to do what you should. Otherwise, you should fear that after preaching to others you might be disqualified" (1 Corinthians 9:25).

There was a great noise as new angels and glorified people came near. I wondered what was taking place, when the man informed me. "The Lord has commissioned His servants to build a new home for His new citizen" (John 14:2). Then he asked, "Would you like to witness how our lives in the heavenly city are shaped by our decisions on earth?"

I nodded in approval and my guides led the way. I was

reminded once again of the teaching of Jesus Christ, as I walked the city and appraised the various mansions. "In My Father's house," Jesus Christ promised, "there are many mansions, if it were not so, I would have told you. I go to prepare a place for you" (John 14:2).

I was led to a mansion on the outer limits of the city. Outside it gleamed with light and inside lived a man, who had once swayed the masses with his preaching. He was considered great on earth and had acquired much wealth for himself in the process. He had preached to thousands that his wealth was a sign of God's blessing and all should seek the same on earth (3 John 1:2). Therefore, when the door opened I was surprised, for the mansion seemed sparse, even frugal. The man sat in a wide padded armchair. He stood up and hugged me. I didn't know his name, yet I knew he was once famous.

"It is a real privilege to meet you," I confirmed.

"It is a joy to be in the Master's glory," was his reply.

"May I ask why you live in such a sparse mansion?"

"In my life, I believed hoarding wealth was my duty (Luke 12:16-40). It proved to others that I was what I proclaimed – a real man of God!" Then he laughed at himself. "How foolish was I!"

I questioned him. "Are you being punished?"

"There is no punishment in heaven," he said. "There are rewards and to each is given what was promised" (Matthew 20:1-16).

"You must be sad that others have more than you?" I suggested.

"There is no sadness in heaven. I live in the Master's light and glory. In that glory, all else is as nothing."

"If you could do it all again what would you change?" I inquired.

"I stored up riches on earth where they faded away," he said. "I should have stored up treasure in heaven" (Matthew 6:2).

"Everyone needs a home, food and clothing," I blurted out. "It is biblical to provide for our own (Proverbs 13:22, 1 Timothy 5:8). How can I know how much to spend on myself and what to give to God?"

"The true measure of a man is determined not by what he owns," he summarised, "but by what he chooses not to own. Consider what the Master said to the rich young ruler: 'If you want to be perfect, go, sell what you have and give to the poor, and you will have treasure in heaven; and follow Me' (Matthew 19:21). The Lord was testing his heart to expose his true first love!"

The angel guided me outside of the house and we began to

walk silently from the outer limits towards the centre of the city. As we moved I thought about what this man had said, "The true measure of a man is determined not by what he owns, but by what he chooses not to own." What did he mean? I think he was trying to tell me that people who choose not to own, what they can afford, are closer to God than those who embrace the world's love of consumer wealth. Many have overstretched their incomes to embrace an unsustainable consumer lifestyle; and it is good when people live below their means, so from their overflow others can be blessed.

I suddenly recalled Christians whom I knew with various levels of income that lived simple lifestyles. They had once been a mystery to me and now I knew they were close to the Kingdom. Then there were the pensioners and the hard-working families, all who gave sacrificially to God's Kingdom. The widow's mite is like dynamite in the Kingdom! God does not measure how much we give, but what it costs us to give (Mark 12:41-44). What we keep for self, is as important as what we give (Luke 6:38, James 4:17).

"There is a principle taught in Scripture," the man told me as we walked, "The more you keep for yourself in life, the less you have in eternity. You can only keep what you give away" (Matthew 6:19-21, Luke 16:25, Hebrews 11:26, 1 Timothy 6:19).

"Everyone needs a home, transport, clothes, food and so forth," I argued defensively. "We are called by God to save for the future and provide for our own!" (Proverbs 13:22, 1 Timothy 5:8).

"It's amazing how your grandparents' generation lived on so little, yet gave so much to get the gospel to others," the angel declared as he interrupted us with care. "They sent the gospel to the nations because they knew the difference between a want and a need. You give because you hope God will give you something in return. They gave because they loved Christ by their deeds" (James 2:20).

I wanted to defend my position, yet I knew the angel was making an honest point and it was cutting deep into my comfort zone. In previous generations, the list of 'needs' or 'necessities' in life were relatively few; but from the 1960s onwards many 'wants' were renamed 'needs,' to such an extent that we no longer know the difference! Meanwhile, as the 'rich' church became prosperous it gave less and less towards fulfilling the Great Commission (Mark 16:15-18, Revelation 3:17-20). It seems that the more God gave to us, the less we did for Him, as we kept more for selfish desires.

"You have been blessed to be a blessing," the man told me.

"You have not received from God to indulge yourself. You are called to crucify the flesh and love, not in words but by action (1 John 3:17). How can the love of God dwell in your heart, if you do not care about the lost – the very ones Christ gave His life for? Do you really have the Spirit of God in you? You have not been a blessing to others because you have become lost in the swamp of self. You have not released God's help to others, you have hindered it (James 4:4-5). You seek wealth believing it will make you happy; whilst it is more blessed to give than to receive" (Acts 20:35).

"I find your message very challenging," I acknowledged.

"This is milk," he insisted. "Would you like James to teach you? He wrote: 'Come now you rich, weep and howl for the miseries that are coming upon you! Your riches are corrupted and your garments are moth-eaten. Your gold and your silver are corroded, and their corrosion will be a witness against you and will eat your flesh like fire. You have heaped up treasure in the last days...You have lived on the earth in pleasure and luxury' " (James 5:1-5).

"I've never heard that preached in my church," I said defensively.

"Have you heard this?" the man asked. "Do not store up treasure on earth, where moths and rust destroy, and where thieves break in and steal. Store your treasures in heaven where moths and rust cannot destroy, and thieves do not break in and steal. Where your treasure is, there your heart will also be" (Matthew 6:19-21).

"Is He your Lord?" he asked. "If you answer yes, why do you not follow His teaching?"

I couldn't answer him. I had never comprehended how far away my thoughts had been from God. It is biblical to be responsible with money (Proverbs 13:22, 1 Timothy 5:8), but I had been selfish and was taught by preachers to be so! (2 Timothy 4:3). I was living for this world, with my desires aimed solely at worldly longings.

"For no one can lay any foundation other than the one we already have in Jesus Christ," he said. "Anyone who builds on that foundation may use a variety of materials, gold, silver, jewels, wood, hay, or straw. But in the judgment, the fire will reveal what kind of work each builder has done. The fire will show if a person's work has any value. If the work survives, that builder will receive a reward. If the work is burned up, the builder will suffer great loss. The builder will be saved, but like someone barely escaping through a wall of flames" (Mark 9:49, 1

Corinthians 3:11-15).

As the man read this to me, I considered the preacher I met who lived sparsely in heaven and I knew he had been through this fire. On earth, his work looked very good; but tested by God it was burned up. He had suffered loss, whilst still being saved. On the edges of the city, I saw many other mansions where people lived. They had joy, but they too lost their rewards by foolish living.

"Please explain what happened to the people who now live in the sparse mansions of heaven," I said. "I don't want to be like them."

"The Lord explained this clearly. He said, 'If you ignore the least commandment and teach others to do the same, you will be called the least in the Kingdom of Heaven. But anyone who obeys God's laws and teaches them will be called great in the Kingdom of Heaven' (Matthew 5:19). Those who suffered loss in the fire are the ones who taught people to love this world. They were saved, but their lifestyles testified against them. They ignored the teaching of the Lord and encouraged others to do the same; this is why they are called the least in the Kingdom. But do not fear, for the least in the greatest Kingdom eternity has ever known is still great!"

We walked for hours toward the city centre. As we drew closer to its heart, we found many greater mansions and rewarded people.

"Who are the ones who live in these mansions?" I asked.

"These were the least on earth," he announced. "The Lord said, 'But many who seem to be important now will be the least important then and those who are considered least here will be the greatest then' " (Matthew 19:30).

In the city, all had heavenly bodies and I could no longer see their former nationalities. Then, the angel touched my shoulder and I was able to see their past once again. As we walked closer to the heart of the city, many lived there that came from Africa, Asia, South America and the Pacific. These were the forgotten ones, the people who had lived on a pittance, yet had sacrificed the widow's mite for the Lord (Mark 12:42). They had once lived in mud huts and ramshackle tin homes; now they resided in the best mansions. The last is truly the first in heaven!

I was reminded of the words of Jesus when He prepared for the Great Supper. Many who were invited made excuses so they could enjoy their short-lived passing pleasures and so He told His servants: "Go out quickly into the streets and lanes of the city and bring in the poor and maimed, and the lame and the blind.

For I say to you that none of those who were invited shall taste My supper" (Luke 14:21-24).

These words were being partially fulfilled in the heavenly city and I was also given insight into the beatitudes of Matthew 5. On earth, the opposite of this teaching often seemed to be true; yet now the poor in spirit had inherited the Kingdom; those who mourned were comforted and those who hungered for righteousness were filled.

As I kept walking inwards I found the homes of former slaves, of prisoners of Christ and the martyrs. There were Romans from the second century, living next door to twentieth-century Chinese Christians who were tortured for Christ and died in prison.

I was invited into one person's mansion and inside was the most wonderful furniture. Once again I thought: 'This is perfect, why didn't we think of this before?' On the wall was a verse recalling those who had overcome the extreme persecution of their faith:

'For you had compassion on me in my chains and joyfully accepted the plundering of your goods, knowing that you have a better and an enduring possession for yourselves in heaven' (Hebrews 10:34).

I had a conversation with the owner, and he explained how his dedication to Christ had led to his home being taken and his goods being plundered; now he was rewarded (Matthew 19:29). He explained how the disciples never desired riches because they lived for eternity and refused the symbols of human prestige.

"Did the disciples desire to dress like Caesar or ride around in a chariot?" he asked. "Did they want temporal treasure when most had never heard of Christ? Did they seek recognition by what they owned, or by the Divine Spirit who owned them? (1 Corinthians 4:9-16). Remember, you are not your own, for you were bought at a price" (1 Corinthians 6:20).

He reminded me of the Lord's teaching of the spiritual calibre of John the Baptist. Jesus said, "What did you go out to see? A man clothed in soft garments? Indeed those who are gorgeously apparelled and live in luxury are in kings' courts" (Luke 7:25).

The man told me that John was a prophet who had died to the self-indulgences of the carnal nature, and in the ministry of all the prophets, they never sought the accolades and rewards of fame. Daniel proved that gold and silver had no hold on him (Daniel 5:16-17). Elisha was offered wealth by Naaman after he was healed and the prophet said, "I will receive nothing." This prophet did not want his ministry or the testimony of this new convert to be tainted by greed, and when his servant betrayed him he asked, "Is it time to receive money?" God judged the servant's greed (2 Kings 5:16-26).

I was directed to James 2:5 and to read it out loud:

"Listen, my beloved brethren, has God not chosen the poor of this world to be rich in faith and heirs of the Kingdom which He promised to those that love Him?"

I thought heaven would be like a holiday for me; nevertheless, I was being challenged in a way no preacher ever achieved. My world was turned upside down and I was shocked by the claims of Christ on my life, which had been ignored for years!

The man waved goodbye to me as I left his mansion and on the golden streets there were many others from previous generations. I saw believers from every age, including the Middle Ages and from every region where the gospel has been preached.

I then met a British woman from the twentieth century, a rarity in this part of the city and asked, "Why do you live here?"

"I also lived for Christ and Him alone," she stated. "There is some born poor who live to the Lord and others who are rich, who live fully for Him. I gave up much for Him and He gave me a great reward."

"Is it a sin to be rich on earth?" I inquired.

"Those who are rich can help others hear the gospel," she stated. "There is no sin in having wealth, but it is a sin to withhold it from God's Kingdom. All people are stewards of the gifts and talents God has given to them, and if they use them for their selfish desires, beware the judgment! (Matthew 25:14-30, 2 Corinthians 5:10). Think about what James wrote: 'To him who knows to do good and does not do it, to him it is sin' (James 4:17).

"Every person receives their gift from God above," she added. "Did you not heed the parable of the coins and the call to invest in God's work? (Luke 19:12-27). In your land some are given the ability to succeed in the best-paid careers and to earn a large wage; others are given limited abilities. All are expected to invest their time, skills, gifts and money for the Master's use. Those who give will receive and those who withhold lose all. Jesus' teaching is not complicated: 'To whom much has been given much will be required' " (Luke 12:48).

By this point in the conversation, I was squirming by the thought-provoking examples I received. I enjoyed seeing the beauty of heaven; however, I did not want to change my life on earth! Yet, I realised I must, because it would be selfish for me to indulge in this experience and not help others to come to heaven!

"Let me tell you of my great joy in the Lord," she added. "Each day in heaven I walk the streets and meet people whom I introduced to the Lord Jesus. I obeyed the Lord and it was costly; I became a channel for Him to reach others with the gospel and now in heaven, I never regret the price I paid for serving Him" (Philippians 4:1).

"How did you give up so much of yourself to Christ?" I asked.

"The ecstasy of His love leads the will to desperate undertakings," she replied. "Nevertheless, I know of many others on earth who did not endure; those who failed to run their race to the very end (1 Corinthians 9:24, Hebrews 12:1). Do you know why they failed to be faithful? It was because they did not keep eternity in mind. They did not think of heaven as a real place, as their final home. They forgot the call of Christ in their heart because they were lost in the cares of life (Mark 4:19, Luke 8:14, 21:34). When heaven is as real to you as it is in the Bible, it will give you the strength to endure to the end."

"We can't all be famous missionaries," I insisted. "Most of us live very common simple lives. There are bills to be paid!"

"Do you see that woman over there?" she asked, pointing her out.

I nodded feeling unable to speak in this challenging environment. "She lived a small life in an overlooked town in the central USA. Life was tough and she gave sacrificially to the Lord, whom she loved with all her heart. She helped get the gospel to the unreached around the world because she denied self to sow into the Kingdom. Every day as she worked, she spent time in prayer and she now lives at the heart of the city. The qualifications to live here is not about how much you give of your wealth, rather how much you give of yourself. This is the lesson of the widow's mite and the rich young ruler. It was not money the young man held back from the Lord; it was his heart – What about you?" (Luke 21:3, Romans 12:1).

Chapter Eleven

A Matter of the Will

I entered another section of the New Jerusalem, still battling in my heart and struggling over these conversations. How could I live up to these high and holy standards? How could I match the sacrifice of those who had given all to the Lord, or to poor believers who gave up the little they had for Him?

The angel and the man guided me through the broad streets and pointed out items of interest, as they witnessed my inner struggle.

"Only you can decide to surrender all you have to the Lord," the man told me. "No-one will force you; however if you choose to become like the widow who helped Elijah, who gave her last meal to the Lord, He can multiply it for your sake and others. She did not give away all she had foolishly; she simply made it available to the Lord and He chose where and what to give" (1 Kings 17:1-24).

"You ask me for works?"

"No," he answered, "the Lord asks for your heart and where your heart is, there your treasure is also (Luke 12:34). If you treasure anything more than God, the only way you can prove you are fully His, is to give it to Him and allow God to take it. He may give it back or He may not" (Genesis 22: 9-12, 1 Kings 19:19-21).

"It would have been easier for me if the Lord had asked for service, rather than my heart," I replied. "With service, I can pick and choose what I want to give to Him, and I will still be free from being His bondslave (Romans 12:1, 1 Corinthians 7:21-22, 9:19). Yet if I give Him all my heart, He must become the Lord of every area of my life!"

"You can be a slave to sin in this life (John 8:34), or a son and heir (Galatians 4:7), with the promise of a crown," he replied. "Many choose to offer their service to the Lord, instead of their heart."

"Service is good," I stated to justify my inner struggle.

"Service can never replace citizenship," the man answered. "Many substitute good works for a living relationship with Christ. They seek to do good works to find God's will for their lives, instead of finding God's will and intimacy with Him, which leads to good works."

The angel had the Bible held open to Ephesians and pointed again to a passage which he wanted me to read. I must confess I did not want to read another passage because these words were cutting into my second-rate Christianity. God's Word was like a hammer smashing the hard rock of my heart and like a fire burning up the dross of my life (Jeremiah 23:29). His Word was like a sword dividing my soul and proving the inadequacy, superficiality and shallowness of my faith (Hebrews 4:12).

"For we are His workmanship," I read reluctantly, "created in Christ Jesus for good works which God prepared beforehand that we should walk in them" (Ephesians 2:10).

The angel announced compassionately, "How can you walk in the plans and purposes of God for your life if you are busy with works, seeking to prove to yourself and others you are sincere?"

"You must seek the Lord first," the man added, "then out of that close and intimate relationship with the Holy Spirit, He will direct you into the good works, which He has created for you in Christ Jesus. If you seek your own ministry and works, you will serve yourself believing that God is pleased. How can He be pleased with you when you are serving out of wrong motives and disobeying Him?"

"So," I said arrogantly, "I have to 'feel' led before I do anything?"

"The gift of feelings was given by God to compliment your life, not to dominate it," he answered. "There will be many times when you must exercise lordship over your feelings. You must master them and they are not to master you. Your feelings should follow your faith led decisions, not the other way around."

In confusion, I said, "What is faith, if it is separate from feelings?"

"Faith is not exercised primarily by your mind or by your emotions. Some say they do not feel God – what has a feeling got to do with God? Is God subject to human feelings? Faith is more than that! How you feel should not have any say in matters of faith. Faith is a matter of the will. You have to exercise your will to believe in God. You must set your will to believe and act accordingly. Faith is the answer when there is no answer. It is the substance of things hoped for, the evidence of things not seen" (Hebrews 11:1).

"How can I exercise faith?" I inquired feeling out of my depth.

"You exercise faith when you step out into the unknown and trust in God alone wherever He leads. Your faith is stretched when you walk so close to God, that you hear the voice of the Holy Spirit leading and directing, and you obey. Exercising faith is when you come out into the deep and walk on the water into the unknown."

The angel added, "You have laughed at Peter as he sunk in the water, yet you have not tried to walk on a puddle!" (Mark 14:29-31).

"How can I walk on water when there is no sea in heaven?" I asked, as I laughed without levity (Revelation 21:1). The angel suddenly took a step forward and rebuked me in his mercy.

"You ask questions and you do not listen to the answers (Mark 8:18). You seek for the sake of seeking. You want to tell others what you have seen and heard because of pride."

I began to sulk at this challenge and thought to myself: 'Why does this angel not like me?' I wished I had left heaven in the fields of paradise because I was now being challenged greatly in the city.

"My son, do not despise the discipline of the Lord," read the man from the Scriptures, "nor be discouraged when you are rebuked. For whom the Lord loves He chastens and scourges every son whom He receives" (Hebrews 12:5-6).

That Word helped me. The angel is a servant of God and he reproved me because God desires for me to stand in faith, and be transformed into a greater reflection of Christ. Besides, deep in my heart, I knew the angel was right. I had judged the angel harshly because he spoke the truth to me. I also recalled in the Bible that angels do not respond very well to lack of faith! How can they be in the presence of God one minute and then have a 'debate' with an unbelieving carnal human the next? I recalled that Moses' unbelief almost cost him his life and the father of John the Baptist was struck dumb when he doubted what an angel told him (Exodus 4:24-27, Luke 1:5-20). By the standards of the Bible, I was being treated with outstanding patience by this angel, and I did myself no favours with my constant questioning, self-justification and doubting.

"The sea was a dangerous way to travel in the ancient world," the man said, interrupting my thoughts. "The ancients needed the sea to move goods around and it separated the peoples. In heaven, there is no more sea because there is no more separation. There is one body in Christ (Romans 12:5). The peoples whom you once thought of as being from a faraway land will share the heavenly city with you, as brothers and fellow citizens. Come and I will show you."

Perhaps his kind words suggested I was forgiven for my outburst? I dared not ask, so I followed the angel and the man, as they led me to a new section of the city. In this area, the people of the neighbourhood waited for me. They had heavenly bodies and I knew in my spirit they were Chinese on earth.

One of them came to me, embraced me and said, "We are citizens of heaven because your friend made it possible for us to hear!"

I knew exactly who they meant. They spoke of a friend from church, who often talked about making small sacrifices to help reach the world with the gospel. He encouraged me to sacrifice something and to live a simpler lifestyle in response to the Lord's final command (Mark 16:15-18). He unsubscribed from many non-essential bills to help finance indigenous evangelists. He kept telling me it would cost £16/$25 a month (in 2020) to help aid one local evangelist to preach to the unreached, yet I had been cynical about his plea. He often quoted this Scripture: 'That now your (financial) abundance may supply their lack, that their abundance (of converts) may supply your lack' (2 Corinthians 8:14).

"Your friend supported the Chinese evangelist who came to our village and preached the gospel," one told me. "We are part of the works that are accounted to him in heaven" (Revelation 14:13).

I had often been blasé about my friend's lifestyle and searched for reasons to avoid helping. Can I afford it? Would my money get wasted? Would they preach 'my' doctrines etc? Yet, in the light of the glory of heaven, I realised all my excuses were a smokescreen to avoid the taxing call in my spirit: "What will you do my child? Will you play your part in reaching every creature with the gospel?"

I couldn't preach in China or other nations, but I could help support a Chinese evangelist and the sacrifice was relatively small. However, I did not want to give! My Christian faith was self-seeking! "What will God do for me?" was my question! But now with these Chinese brethren before me, I knew that real people's eternal lives were being changed by my friend's choice to get involved! I had wasted so much of my time and money on self, whereas he had stored up treasures in heaven (Matthew 6:20).

I spent hours being greeted by the members of this neighbourhood and felt overwhelmed by their kindness. They thanked me for my support and I was embarrassed because I had done nothing to help get the gospel to them! My friend had given to a ministry that releases the finances to support the evangelist who reached them and he paid for the Bibles they could not afford. He will be rewarded for this 'fruit' in heaven

(John 4:35-37, Philippians 4:17).

I had followed a 'bless me, self seeking' form of Christianity and now I met the fruit of those who obeyed the last command of Christ (Matthew 28:18-20). How could I tell these Chinese believers I had spent so much on gadgets and clothes, which are now obsolete or out of fashion, and had given nothing to help get the gospel to them! I claimed to follow Christ, whilst refusing to heed His final call!

Jesus constantly spoke of preparing for eternity and I had hardly even begun to think about His message. Life on earth is not the end – it is the preparation for real life. The first page in an eternal book.

The angel opened his mouth again to ask me another question and I was afraid of what he would say next. My inner thoughts and selfish motives were being exposed by the probing questions, and I feared learning how ineffectual and carnal 'my faith' was.

"What would you give if you really believed the gospel is true?" he asked. "How much would you sacrifice if you truly believed mankind is forever lost, and God came in human form to suffer and die for them, so they could be redeemed? What changes in your life would you make if you were convinced that God died on the cross and was raised again on the third day?" (Matthew 17:23).

I felt insulted by these questions, saying, "I do believe!"

"No, you don't," he insisted in a whisper.

"Mankind is lost in sin, weighed down by iniquity and it will drag them to hell. However, God put on human flesh and suffered in the place of His creation. He was born into the weakness of man, suffered cruelly and was crucified. Have you ever heard of such a thing? He did not suffer for angels, but for mankind who He created out of the dust (Hebrews 1:5-13). He died and was raised again in victory, and was given the keys to death and hell. Now what is required is for every creature to be given the opportunity to hear of Christ's death and resurrection – so they may put their faith in Him!"

"I believe this to be true," I insisted.

"No, you don't," he asserted. "If you truly believed it would change your life. How could you live the life you have been living if you believed? How could you do so little to help spread the gospel to the world if you believed? Do you really believe you could be filled with the Holy Spirit and at the same time be indifferent to Jesus' final command to make disciples of all nations? If you are indifferent, it is because you are full of self, not God."

"I'm a church member and in the choir!" I replied. "I tithe and I volunteer to help in the children's club. I do believe!"

"Please heed the wisdom of the Scriptures," he replied, "if indeed you do believe! 'If you confess with your mouth the Lord Jesus and believe in your heart that God has raised Him from the dead you will be saved...For whoever calls on the name of the Lord will be saved. How then shall they call on Him in whom they have not believed? And how shall they believe in Him of whom they have not heard? And how shall they hear without a preacher? And how shall they preach unless they are sent?' (Romans 10:9, 13-15).

"The three 'and how' in these Scriptures end with – and how will you respond to this revelation from God? What will you do? So, I ask you once more: What would you give if you truly believed?

"Jesus said, 'The harvest is truly great but the labourers are few; therefore pray the Lord of the harvest to send out labourers' (Luke 10:2). Here you are commanded to pray a prayer that you can help answer. The harvest is ready. Will you help send a labourer?"

I knew I had a choice to make when I returned to earth. I could continue to live for self and my selfish desires, or I could make a relatively small sacrifice to enable one home-grown indigenous evangelist to be free to evangelise his or her own people in Asia or another unreached continent.

Did I want to spend eternity knowing I wasted all I had on my desires or did I too want to meet people in heaven who were saved because I helped someone to preach the gospel in a land where I could not? No longer could I ignore the command of Christ. I chose in my heart that somewhere in the world, someone would be sharing the gospel of Jesus because I acted and helped. Finally, I took Christ's last command seriously.

Chapter Twelve

Back To Eden

On this journey I felt the glory of heaven; nevertheless, in its pure light, I saw the selfishness of my heart (Jeremiah 17:9). In my church many would have testified that I was a deeply committed believer who studied the Bible, prayed and tried to help others; but now in this purity, everything I had done seemed to be selfish in motive. I had given to receive, I loved to be seen and I prayed for the reward of others hearing me (Matthew 6:5-7).

I then understood why men of God chastised themselves saying, "Woe is me, for I am undone (Isaiah 6:5). Woe is me, for I am a selfish man (Jeremiah 15:10). O wretched man that I am; who can save me from this body of death?" (Romans 7:24).

"Jesus Christ can save you from yourself," the man said as the angel stood still (Romans 7:25). "But to be saved from yourself, you must first understand where this selfish root within you found its genesis."

Suddenly a blast of wind struck me and I was taken on a journey like that of Ezekiel. I felt the hand of the Lord come upon me and He brought me out in the Spirit and set me down in the midst of Eden (Ezekiel 37:1). I did not know if it was ancient Eden or its reflection.

Eden was set at a perfect temperature. I felt the strength of the sun warming me and the shade regulated. The garden was different from paradise because it was comparable to a South American rainforest, with a delicate balance of plant life and with light bouncing through the trees in various areas. There was no rain.

I breathed in and the smell reminded me of the mist of early morning (Genesis 2:9), as the glory of the light shone, bounced and reflected through Eden. There were trees of every shape and size, which are pleasant to the sight and good for food. There was a river whose source was unknown and it flowed out of Eden to water the garden (Genesis 2:10).

I imagined Adam working here so very long ago. He had to tend the garden and I could tell it had been a pleasant job, varied inactivity and joyous to the soul. God had given him the task of naming all the animals, birds and beasts. All was in harmony and became subject to him under God's supervision. The creative nature of God had been sown into Adam's soul and out of that deep source within, he was able to name all that was before him (Genesis 2).

"What do you see?" asked the angel (Jeremiah 1:11, Amos 7:8).

"I see Eden in its glory," I replied.

"Do you know what was lost in Eden?"

I was beginning to learn that each time I was asked a question, it was not because the angel did not know the answer, but because I needed to know it. Technically, I may have known the answer and yet they had never been revealed in me. I knew them at a distance, but they never penetrated my heart leading to a real change.

I recalled what preachers had taught about the account of Eden, which is found in the first few chapters of Genesis. The serpent in Genesis 3:1-5, is the embodiment of Satan and his primary activity was to deceive the first two humans, Adam and Eve.

Satan is crafty and sought to encourage Adam and Eve to question God, which led to doubt and rebellion. After they had dwelt on the questions Satan asked, they both fell into sin and the world fell with them. What were the many consequences of this fall?

Adam and Eve used their free will, not to love God as they should have, but to rebel and their fellowship with God was violently broken. Without understanding it, they sided themselves with the greatest rebel Satan (Genesis 3:6), and were then expelled from the paradise of Eden (Genesis 3:24, Luke 10:18).

One consequence of their sin was they both lost the beauty and protection of godly innocence. They had once only known good, and now their eyes were opened and they understood evil as well (Genesis 3:7, 22). This evil resulted in severe damage to the relationship between Adam and Eve. There was a loss of trust and purity between the sexes, as lust entered the world, and they became subject to fear, embarrassment and shame (Genesis 3:8). Instead of exercising responsibility to guard each other against the enemy, Adam and Eve assigned blame (Genesis 3:12-13).

Adam and Eve's eternal and spiritual life source was also cut off. They became like batteries which would never be recharged. As a result, their physical bodies and minds became subject to sickness and old age (Genesis 3:19). They had been created in glory from the dust; now they would return to the dust in dishonour (Genesis 3:19, 1 Corinthians 15:43).

The reproductive process was also subject to pain: Men would now be birthed in sorrow and women would suffer in childbirth. Women also lost the equality that God intended (Genesis 3:16).

Adam once worked in a carefree manner and now life would become a battle for survival. The pleasant exercise of work was now demanding and with great effort, and by the sweat of his brow would he eat. There would be 'thorns and thistles' in all forms at work, and everything hard, unpleasant, produces strain, demands labour, leads to frustration and stress was born (Genesis 3:17-19).

God had also given Adam and Eve authority over the earth, but they gave their authority to the serpent, replacing the Kingship of God over their lives with the kingship of Satan. He became the god of this world (2 Corinthians 4:4), and they became unknowing slaves in Satan's kingdom. They became slaves of sin (John 8:34), and futility in every area of their lives was the result.

The great tragedy was that as Adam and Eve fell from grace, we also fell with them. Their sinful nature became our sinful nature.

"Is there no hope of a return to the glory of Eden?" I asked the angel.

"Have you studied what was revealed to the apostles?" he asked.

The Bible opened to Paul's description of these events: "The first man Adam became a living being, the second (Christ) became a life-giving spirit. The first man was of the earth, made of dust; the second Man is the Lord from heaven' (1 Corinthians 15:45-47). For as in Adam all die, even so in Christ all shall be made alive (1 Corinthians 15:22)...our Lord Jesus Christ, who gave Himself for our sins, that He might deliver us from this present evil age, according to the will of our God and Father" (Galatians 1:3-4).

"In heaven, all the consequences of the sin of Adam and Eve will be undone and more," the angel prophesied and as he spoke the plants in the garden shook, as if they heard (Romans 8:19-22).

Suddenly, my spiritual eyes were opened and I witnessed a pure river of life, clear as crystal flowing from the great city in the heavens. The water flooded into Eden and it poured in with such intensity that it soon came up to my waist. I looked up into heaven and on the streets of the city, and on either side of the river, was the tree of life, which bore twelve fruits, each tree yielding its fruit every month. The leaves of the tree were for the healing of the nations (Revelation 22:1-5). The curse of Adam was broken and healing flowed from heaven to the new earth. With this revelation, I shot like a thunderbolt from Eden back into the heavenly Jerusalem.

"Adam and his wife ate in disobedience of the first tree of life and were cursed," I concluded (Genesis 2:9, 22-24). "Who will get to eat of the second tree of life and be blessed with the healing of the Second Adam?"

Several scriptures were brought into my mind and I repeated them, "To him who overcomes I will give to eat from the tree of life, which is in the midst of the paradise of God (Revelation 2:7). Blessed are those who do His commandments, that they may have the right to the tree of life and may enter through the gates into the city" (Revelation 22:14).

"Those who may eat of the second tree of life must obey the commandments of God," said the angel, "and the great command is to believe on the Lord Jesus Christ and be saved (Acts 8:37, 16:31). Then, out of their close relationships with God, they must choose to overcome in Him. Those who put their faith in Christ's death and resurrection will receive His righteousness by faith and, 'The fruit of the righteous is a tree of life and he who wins souls is wise' (Proverbs 11:30). Therefore winning people to the Lord is always wise and 'a wholesome tongue is a tree of life, but perverseness in it breaks the spirit' (Proverbs 15:4).

"What of the devil?" I asked the angel. "Will he be judged for leading Adam and Eve into sin?"

"He was and will be judged," the angel confirmed.

I was then shown the judgments of Satan which are chronicled in the book of Revelation. Then, the angel touched me and I shot like lightning back through 'time,' and I stood in a court of glorious light, unable to see, but I could hear all that was said.

"Thus says the Lord God," said a voice like thunder, as I was blinded by the penetrating light. "You were the seal of perfection, full of wisdom and perfect in beauty. You were in Eden, the garden of God; every precious stone was your covering: The sardius, topaz and diamond, beryl, onyx, and jasper, sapphire, turquoise, and emerald with gold. The workmanship of your timbrels and pipes was prepared for you on the day you were created. You were the anointed cherub who covers; I established you."

My eyes had only slightly adjusted to the light and through the mist and haze, I saw the back of a large throne and a dark shadowy figure stood in front, quaking in fear – a defeated foe. It was Satan! (Revelation 12:9)

"You were on the holy mountain of God," I heard. "You walked back and forth amid fiery stones. You were perfect in your ways from the day you were created, till iniquity was found in you...You became filled with violence within and you sinned. Therefore I cast you out as a profane thing, out of the mountain of God and I destroyed you, O covering cherub, from the midst of the fiery stones. Your heart was lifted up because of your beauty. You corrupted your wisdom for the sake of your splendour. I cast you to the ground" (Ezekiel 28:13-17).

I was reminded that Jesus also witnessed this event in heaven for He said, "I saw Satan fall like lightning from heaven" (Luke 10:18).

Chapter Thirteen

Calvary

"May I see how Satan was judged after this account?" I asked.

"Defeating the enemy was not cheap or easy," the man declared.

I was taken to what appeared as first century Jerusalem. There was a great commotion in the city and I witnessed a crowd, with a man in the centre being whipped before them.

"Please don't show me this," I said, as I turned my face away. "I know the story and seeing it will be terrible."

"Are you afraid of the truth?" the man said, adding, "We see Jesus, who was made a little lower than the angels, for the suffering of death crowned with glory and honour, that He by the grace of God might taste death for everyone" (Hebrews 2:9).

"I wanted to see Satan judged," I indicated.

"He became flesh and blood," the man replied, "that through death, He might destroy him who had the power of death, that is the devil, and release those who through fear of death were all their lifetime subject to bondage" (Hebrews 2:14-15).

A Roman soldier lifted his whip and swung it striking Jesus. My body jerked. It was the most terrible sound I had ever heard. The whip struck again and I turned to find a dense crowd blocking the view, as the soldier lifted his arm again and swung.

I crouched down and in between the people I was able to see two arms tied around a post, and blood was dripping down His arms onto His hands. Jesus' hands were clenched and when He was struck they instantly flung open with His fingers pointing outwards, as if He was trying to throw the pain away, and they clenched again. The soldier kept whipping Him and I was unable to watch.

"I have read of this many times," I said, "it's too hard to watch."

"You have become too familiar with the account of the Lord's death, without acknowledging the cost to Him, or the implications for you," I was told. "For none of them can by any means redeem his brother, nor give to God a ransom for him. For the redemption of their souls is costly" (Psalm 49:7-8).

This was torture, a gross act of cruelty; it disturbed me to such an extent that my eyes watered and I thrust my hands over my ears.

"Please make it stop," I begged, as I jerked with each strike.

"This is the past," he said. "It has happened and you have been called to remember this in breaking bread" (1 Corinthians 11:23-28).

Then, the angel touched me and he pulled me through 'space' to the place of crucifixion. I stood in the distance and I could see three crosses; I was not close enough to see the strain on the face of Christ, who was now on the cross.

I then discovered why I was so far away; just before me, I saw some of the disciples running for their lives away from the cross.

"Many want to be with the resurrected Lord," the man told me, "but few want to go with Him to die in shame at Calvary" (Mark 8:34, Hebrews 13:13).

"But the women never left Him," added the angel. "Look and see."

By comparison to the man whom I talked with, the angel had said far fewer words; yet everything he had said was of great significance. I pondered his statement and it struck me that it must have been comforting to the Lord, that the women did not abandon Him. The men had made great promises indicating they would stand with Jesus till the end, yet it was the women who kept the faith in the darkest hour (Luke 23:27), and assisted Him daily (Luke 8:33).

"Thank God the women stayed with Him," I said to the angel.

"Isaiah witnessed His crucifixion in the Spirit," he replied, "and he documented it all." The angel passed me the open Bible and I read: "There is no beauty that we should desire Him. He is despised and rejected. A man of sorrows and acquainted with grief, and we hid, as it were, our faces from Him. Surely He has borne our grief and carried our sorrows. Yet, we esteemed Him stricken, smitten by God and afflicted. But He was wounded for our transgressions. He was bruised for our iniquities. The chastisement of our peace was upon Him and by His stripes, we are healed" (Isaiah 53:2-5).

I looked up at the man and said, "I saw that, by His stripes we are healed. I saw the stripes."

"Read on," said the angel and I returned to reading Isaiah.

"He was oppressed and He was afflicted. He was led as a lamb to the slaughter. Yet it pleased the Lord to bruise Him, He has put Him to grief, when You make His soul an offering for sin. By His knowledge My righteous Servant will justify many, for He shall bear their iniquities. He shall see the labour of His soul and be satisfied. He poured out His soul unto death, and He bore the sin of many and made intercession for the transgressors" (Isaiah

53:7-12).

"It was my sin and of all mankind that crucified Him," I said in shame.

"No," said the angel. "It was His love (1 John 3:16). Greater love has no one than this, than to lay down one's life for his friends (John 15:13). God has demonstrated His love towards mankind, for while you were still sinners – Christ died for you (Romans 5:8), so you could be reconciled to God" (Romans 5:10, 1 Corinthians 15:3, 2 Corinthians 5:19).

"He chose to die," the man continued, "when He could have called twelve legions of angels to save Him" (Matthew 26:53).

In the distance, Christ was hanging on the cross and I felt unable to fully describe all I saw. It was horror and great darkness. I was far away, yet I could see a stain on the ground below the cross, as the blood flowed from His body into the earth. His body was torn by the beating and some cruel men had put a crown of thorns on His head, which was a source of continual agitation and pain.

He was the greatest victim the world has ever known – suffering humiliation, torture and being stripped of all His clothes. In Jerusalem, people had received healing from His hands and those hands were now nailed to wood. The religious leaders openly mocked Him, whilst others expressed hatred at the innocent One.

My eyes were also opened to the spiritual realm and the powers of darkness celebrated; the legions of demons with distorted faces, twisted by their inner misery screamed with brute force. I heard a vile and wicked sound coming from them, as they found sickening respite from their torment as Christ suffered.

Satan was absent because he had entered the body of Judas (Luke 22:3, John 13:27), and Judas' agreement with Satan would lead them both to a very dark end (Matthew 26:24). Judas had the opportunity to have been possessed by God's glory (Ephesians 3:19) but by choosing to rebel and reject the message of Jesus, he was taken over by evil (John 17:12).

The scenes I witnessed were impossible to dwell on, for the sheer horror of Calvary was not bathed in heavenly light.

"Now you understand why the disciples wrote so little about His crucifixion," the man concluded (Matthew 27:35, Mark 15:24-25, Luke 23:33, John 19:18).

"It would hurt too much to describe His crucifixion in detail," I said in agreement. "Even though the cross is central to the faith of Christians, we have tried to turn it into a beautiful symbol; but it is not. The cross was an instrument of horrific prolonged torture."

We sat in silence for the next hours with our view of the three crosses. On seven separate occasions, it appeared those around the cross heard the Lord speaking, and at the last we heard a cry in the distance and His head slumped forward. The city was plunged into darkness and for a moment fear seized me, as if it was the end of the world. There was deep darkness (Matthew 27:46).

I was immediately thrown forward from the place where I sat, as an earthquake shook the area and rocks fell. Then, I heard cries coming from the temple about a disaster inside and a commotion from the tombs, with people shouting the dead were to rise! (Matthew 27:51-54). In excitement and holy fear I drew near to the angel finding strength in his warrior presence.

"The victory is complete," the angel announced, "and now to plunder the enemy!" He touched me on the shoulder and we were thrust downwards towards a great bleak darkness, as we passed into the spiritual world. Our feet landed on a rough substance below and the moments ahead changed with a haze, as a deficiency of light blurred my vision; it all took place with the speed of thunder and lightning.

"For the joy that was set before Him," the angel continued, "He endured the cross, despising its shame" (Hebrews 12:2).

The limited light made it appear I was in a vast cave with the edges of the rock around striking out viciously. I saw so little as I heard the voice of Christ Jesus the Lord echoing in the distance, as He proclaimed to the spirits in prison (1 Peter 3:19-20, 4:6).

I believe I was in a part of hell and it was bleak indeed; but it had no power over Christ and could not hold Him, as the very fabric of Satan's right to power was shaken and broken (Acts 2:27, 31). I heard the thunder of a spiritual war and the screams of the defeated. The enemy had lost his rights and was plundered within and without (Matthew 12:40, Hebrews 2:14, 10:6-7).

I heard the clang of spiritual weapons being surrendered below the feet of Christ as principalities and powers were disarmed, and the heavenly host viewed the demons being humiliated, as a public spectacle was made of them (Colossians 2:15). I witnessed angels in heaven rejoicing, some were dancing, others threw themselves down in worship and cried out, "The wisdom of God...the wisdom of God! He has defeated the enemy through suffering and death. Oh, the wisdom of God! He turns darkness into light and defeat into victory!"

As Judas hung himself, Satan left his body, for the evil one always betrays those who work with him, or agree with his twisted values by their actions (John 6:70, Acts 1:16-18). Satan was unaware of the power of the cross and now it was payback time!

Jesus had descended to plunder Satan's kingdom and dread fell upon Satan (Matthew 25:41). He was soon petrified and exhausted as he sought to gain control. He felt humiliated and very foolish, like a military commander who walked into a trap and cried out, "What is happening?" as his army was plundered (Psalm 68:18).

There was confusion at every level in Satan's kingdom, as the mighty principalities and powers, and the puny demons fled from the holy thunder that shook the darkness. Many demons were taken captive by the angels, to be judged by God in due time and they joined those who were captured in earlier battles (2 Peter 2:4, Jude 1:6, Revelation 12:7-9). This was the beginning of a time of punishment, as those who rebelled were routed (Isaiah 24:21-22).

"He has led captivity captive and gave gifts to men," shouted the angel (Ephesians 4:8). "Freedom from sin, from self and from all demonic power is now made available to those who are bound (Zechariah 9:11). The price had been paid in full for the forgiveness of man's sin! The chains on the hearts of many will break forever!"

I heard some demons whispering to themselves that many people would still want to serve the devil by their works (John 8:44), and this would continue to empower them. However, the enemy had been mortally wounded and would never be able to recover his losses. His days were now numbered and this led to his anger increasing in bitter attacks on all (Revelation 12:12).

As a student of history, I immediately began to compare Satan's predicament with Hitler's in the winter of 1944. Hitler's armies were in retreat on every front and every top military commander knew he had no hope of recovery. Nevertheless, he continued to plan his fantasy empire as if he was winning! He was unwilling to accept what everyone else knew as fact. Hitler was still able to take lives, fire rockets towards Britain and cause great suffering; yet he could never recover. Satan is in a similar position – he can still cause suffering; nevertheless, his absolute future defeat is settled.

Suddenly, the darkness changed to bright light, as we shot through the veil between heaven and earth. I was now in the heavenlies and I saw a trail of fire behind (Ephesians 4:8-10). Demonic beings were screaming, crying and were in retreat in every area. They had been taken by surprise; what they believed was their greatest victory – the death of Christ – had led to their defeat.

Adam in the Garden of Eden had given Satan authority over the earth, but Christ took back the keys forever (Revelation 1:18).

'Having disarmed principalities and powers He made a public spectacle of them, triumphing over them' (Colossians 2:15).

The angel cried out, "The devil has sinned from the beginning and for this purpose the Son of God was manifested, that He might destroy the works of the devil (1 John 3:8); and they overcame him by the blood of the Lamb and by the word of their testimony, and they did not love their lives to the death" (Revelation 12:11).

"Love has conquered all," declared the man. "Through death, He has destroyed him who had the power of death, that is, the devil (Hebrews 2:14). Therefore God has highly exalted Him and given Him the name which is above every name, that at the name of Jesus every knee should bow, of those in heaven, and those on earth, and of those under the earth' (Philippians 2:9-10).

I viewed these past events in a wider context. I saw the crucified Christ walk into a heavenly tabernacle and the Ark of the Covenant was there (Revelation 11:19). The tabernacle on earth was a mere copy of this one, and Christ entered wearing the garments of the High Priest. He did not enter the Most High Place with the blood of goats and calves, but with His own blood, once and for all (Hebrews 8:5, 9:25-28).

I heard another angel cry out, "For if the blood of bulls and goats and the ashes of a heifer, sprinkling the unclean, sanctifies for the purifying of the flesh, how much more shall the blood of Christ, who through the eternal Spirit offered Himself without spot to God, cleanse your conscience from dead works to serve the living God?" (Hebrews 9:11-14).

Then the old tabernacle from earth appeared and a voice announced, "Therefore it was necessary that the copies of the things in the heavens should be purified with the former, but the heavenly things themselves with better sacrifices than these. For Christ has not entered the holy places made with hands, which are copies of the true, but into heaven itself, now to appear in the presence of God for us" (Hebrews 9:23-24).

I wondered if this heavenly tabernacle still stood (Revelation 15:5), was this only a reflection of the past? I knew from John's revelation that there is no temple in heaven, for the Lord God Almighty and the Lamb are its temple (Revelation 21:22).

The mystery of Christ's sacrifice was far too great for me to comprehend (Ephesians 2:16). However, I knew with certainty that the sacrifice of Christ is at the centre of all history (Revelation 5:12, 13:8). Satan is forever defeated by Christ and history is His story.

Chapter Fourteen

The Good Shepherd

This revelation exceeded my expectations and I hardly settled when the man announced, "Where you are going, I cannot come."

A sad countenance came upon me. The man had been a real comfort to me, for he understood human frailty.

"Please come with us," I implored, seeking his company.

"If I go with you I shall not return," he confided. "Paradise and the heavenly city are beautiful; however there is still a greater privilege for you. If I stood where you will soon stand, I would never want to leave; I too can be lost in praise and worship."

I was assured by what he told me and wondered what I would see. What could be so great that even paradise and the heavenly city loses its appeal!

"You have seen the crucified Lord Jesus," announced the angel, "now you must meet the risen and glorified Lord!"

When the angel said those words I trembled and my legs lost their strength, and I fell gently to the ground into a seated position. I had witnessed the Lord's crucifixion from a distance; now I would see Him face to face! (1 Corinthians 13:12).

"Do not be afraid," the angel insisted as he picked me up, "the fear of the Lord is the beginning of wisdom" (Psalm 111:10, Proverbs 1:7, 9:10). I never knew how strong this angel was until now and I was grateful that a bond was forming between us. He had seen me at my worst, for he knew my heart; and it is always the heart that the Lord weighs (1 Samuel 16:7, Matthew 22:37).

"You will need to wear this," the angel told me, as he handed over a robe of righteousness, clean, bright and made of fine linen (Revelation 19:8). It was only when I touched this robe that I became aware how messy my clothes were. I felt embarrassed that I had been walking around wearing torn and dirty rags (Isaiah 64:6).

The Bible indicates the need of being 'clothed' with spiritual clothes; however, I never thought of them as something real, which could be seen by others in the spiritual realm, where we are seated in Christ (Ephesians 2:6). Peter taught we must be 'clothed with humility' (1 Peter 5:5), and we are to 'put on tender mercies, kindness, humility, meekness and long-suffering'

(Colossians 3:12). We are also encouraged to 'put on the whole armour of God' (Ephesians 6:11). On earth, these spiritual clothes are manifested by our godly character and walk of faith. Meanwhile, in the spiritual realm they manifest real power and protection. They are armour!

I had called myself a Christian for a long time; whilst I did not know my spiritual clothes were torn and dirty because I had not 'put on Christ' (Galatians 3:27), nor clothed myself with the fruit of the Spirit (Galatians 5:22). I was like the man James wrote about who studies the Bible and learns that his life is described within, yet forgets. The Scriptures gave him a perfect reflection of his true self; yet as he closed the book of Books, he walked away and forgot what he had learnt (James 1:22-24).

I took the robe from the angel and by faith I put it on and it fitted perfectly. My filthy old clothes were taken from me and were thrown into the fire to be burnt (Jude 23). My robe of righteousness, bought by the blood of Christ Jesus and worn by faith in His life, death and resurrection brought me a sense of authority. I knew I was dressed correctly for the occasion.

The angel beckoned with his hand for me to walk towards the entrance of another room. I took slow steps forward and the echo of my feet touching the floor bounced off the walls.

The doors of a great chamber opened and inside I saw a vast white spacious room, with a thick light blue glory, which appeared as a cloud all around. In my spirit I heard myself thinking, 'Shekinah glory.' Only now did I realise how the Church had been ill-advisedly casual in our declarations of, 'The glory of God is here.' I felt the desire to apologise for our cavalier descriptions of His presence, power and promises; yet in the Shekinah glory, even well-meaning introspection can be of self and must be put to the cross.

In the distance, inside the vast chamber, I saw a figure through the Shekinah cloud (2 Chronicles 5:13-14, 6:1), and He walked towards me through it. The room became dense with glory and it engulfed me, feeling physically heavy. I had to fight to channel my strength to stand up, as the weight made it hard to remain on my feet.

Then the Man walked through the cloud and the figure that was once hidden by the Shekinah became clearer, as His form took shape. I couldn't stand the weight of glory any longer and I dared not view the Man. I suddenly fell onto the floor with my face down and I saw His feet, He stopped in front of me. I couldn't believe my eyes! The One who stood still had human feet which are pierced and He wore sandals (Luke 24:39). There was a lace between the toes and a slider to loosen them.

Two scriptures came to mind: 'Clouds and thick darkness surround Him; righteousness and justice are the foundation of His throne' (Psalm 97:2). 'Like the appearance of a rainbow in the clouds on a rainy day, so was the radiance around Him. This was the appearance of the likeness of the glory of the Lord. When I saw it, I fell facedown and I heard the voice of one speaking' (Ezekiel 1:28).

Suddenly, I felt His hands pull me up! I stood upright, head bowed, my eyes still looking towards the floor. He was still dressed in what I would call a first century Roman tunic. It was woven in one piece without a seam (John 19:23). His garment was shining exceeding white, like snow and was a purity of white unknown to me (Mark 9:3). There was a glow around His body and the energy from His light strengthened me. He raised one arm and with the palm of His hand lifted my chin to look Him in the eyes.

As my eyes moved upward towards His face I prepared my heart to confess all manner of shortcomings. I sensed a flood of tears was going to burst forth. It was not hidden sin which came to my heart, but my frustration that I failed against my best intentions, to live up to His high and holy calling (Romans 7:19, 24-25).

Then my head was raised and He looked into my eyes. I immediately forgot all I was going to say and my moist eyes dried. He had loving and penetrating eyes which knew all and saw all. Those eyes had known and still know sadness. He understood all I had wanted to say and could have said. Further healing took place within me, simply by looking at Him.

There was no need for words. He moved closer to embrace me and I noticed that His hair was pure white. His hands moved towards me and I saw they were still pierced. He hugged me and without speaking any words He welcomed me. I had imagined I would confess much; nevertheless, the time for repentance and confession is on earth (1 John 1:19, Hebrews 9:27).

What can I tell you about His embrace? Oh, the embrace! It was pure love and light. It was power and meekness. I began to understand how the God who created us can design the perfect bliss, which overtakes the soul and transforms it into the ecstasy of love. Imagine planting deep desires within the heart of humankind and fulfilling those desires a thousand times over! He is the embodiment of righteousness, goodness and love.

I met God and He is the best friend any human can have. Christ appeared to me in the form of the Good Shepherd and like

Stephen, I saw the Son of Man (Acts 7:56). He is both the suffering Servant and the glorified Christ together; and when I perceived Him, I beheld the side of Him I needed to see.

In His presence, I felt 'time' shifted resembling slow motion, as if there was a displacement in my perception of 'time.' This later led me to question how this encounter will happen for others. Perhaps Christ will meet us individually in heaven, His presence bends our perception of time. In this case, there will be no queues and He can spend as long as He wants with us individually. Or perhaps we will be thrilled to wait our turn because we have eternity to meet and be with Him. Building expectations of an encounter can be wonderful.

The Lord took me by the arm and led me through a vast door into the clouds, and I walked with Him and I had no fear of falling. The clouds have always been something I have looked up to from earth and I dreamed of walking on them. Did God plant this idea into man's imagination? I wondered if Peter's short walk on the water was a prerequisite to this heavenly leap of faith (Mark 14:28-31). The laws of nature which we are bound by, make walking on clouds impossible, yet in heaven, we are spiritual in nature and the old cannot limit the new.

The clouds are often the domain of Christ (Matthew 26:64, Revelation 1:7, 14:14), and I sat on them, and also walked with the Lord. He spoke to me about many things past, present and things to come; but we did not communicate with words. He thought my thoughts and I thought His. I considered writing down all He shared; however, it was too sacred to transcribe.

My time with the Lord was beautiful and I glowed due to being with Him (Exodus 34:35). In the distance, I watched as my angel came to meet me in the clouds and he beckoned me to join him. The Lord gave His approval and I walked from the clouds back onto the solid ground into the heavenly city.

I was changed by seeing the Lord. Rivers of love flooded into my soul and I felt I never wanted to sin or hurt another again.

The angel held a Bible and it was opened to John's account of one of the Lord's prayers, as Jesus revealed His heart's desire:

"Father, I desire that they also whom You gave Me may be with Me where I am, that they may behold My glory which You have given Me; for You loved Me before the foundation of the world" (John 17:24). I had met the Lord as the Good Shepherd and now as I read this Scripture, I knew He wanted me to see His glory too!

The angel knew my thoughts and led me to another door, high, wide and mighty. It was one hundred feet high and made me feel small. Inscribed on it in the heavenly language was:

'To him who overcomes I will grant to sit with Me on My throne, as I also overcame and sat down with My Father on His throne' (Revelation 2:31).

The doors opened by themselves and I walked through, and behold, we were in the centre of the city and I saw the throne of God (Revelation 22:3-5). Suddenly, there before me was One like a Son of Man, coming with the clouds of heaven. He approached the Ancient of Days and was led into His presence" (Daniel 7:13).

"The throne of God and of the Lamb will be in the city," said a loud voice, "and His servants will serve Him. They will see His face and His name will be on their foreheads. There will be no more night. They will not need the light of a lamp or the light of the sun, for the Lord God will give them light. And they will reign forever and ever" (Revelation 22:3-5).

Seated on the throne next to His Father was Jesus Christ in His glorified state and His countenance was like the sun in its full strength. He wore a gold band around His chest and a flowing garment down to His feet. His eyes were a flame of fire and His feet appeared as fine brass. When He spoke I heard the sound of many waters and out of His mouth came a sharp two-edged sword (Revelation 1:13-16). I could hardly believe the loving Good Shepherd whom I had just met, was also the glorified Son.

There were other smaller thrones and on them were twenty-four elders sitting, clothed in white robes. They wore crowns of gold on their heads (Revelation 4:4). The elders held the prayers of the saints in golden bowls full of incense and there were harps, and they fell before Him singing this song:

"Worthy are You to take the scroll and to open its seals, for You were slain, and by Your blood You ransomed people for God from every tribe and language and people and nation, and You have made them kings and priests to our God, and they shall reign on the earth" (Revelation 5:9-10).

Someone cried out, "There will be a new perfect earth and believers in Christ shall reign," and he continued, "we according to His promise, look for the new heavens and a new earth in which righteousness dwells (2 Peter 3:13). Who amongst us is ready to reign with Christ?"

Responding to this question a multitude of voices praised God and cheered. This made me realise that I had been so transfixed on the Lamb of God and the twenty-four elders, that I overlooked the angels. There were angels everywhere, standing in large legions, divided into ordered ranks. In the distance, there was row after row of mighty warrior angels, clothed in white, majestic in appearance and as bold as lions.

The angels cried out in unison with a loud voice, "Worthy is the Lamb who was slain, to receive power and wealth and wisdom, and might and honour and glory, and blessing! To Him who sits on the throne and to the Lamb, be blessing and honour and glory and might forever and ever" (Revelation 5:11-13).

He who was seated on the throne said, "I will make everything new. I am the Alpha and the Omega, the Beginning and the End. To him who is thirsty, I will give to drink without cost from the spring of the water of life. He who overcomes will inherit all this and I will be his God and he will be My son" (Revelation 21:4-7).

Chapter Fifteen

The Ancient of Days

The glory of Jesus Christ was potent, like the shining sun in full strength; so much so that I was unable with human eyes to perceive the Father in His glory, who sat on His throne (Revelation 22:3-5).

The angel guided me onward and from another vantage point, I was able to glimpse God the Father. Christ was at His right hand (1 Peter 3:22), and there were thunderings, lightnings and shots of fire sent forth from His throne. I only caught a glimpse directly of the Father because the light shining forth made it impossible to glare. I was stunned by His great, royal, solemn and powerful Presence. His voice was deep, rich, honest and true.

On earth, by the power of the Holy Spirit I had said, "Abba Father," to the One on the throne (Romans 8:15, Galatians 4:6); but now the Father was attentive to His many concerns and I dared not interrupt, or seek any personal attention. To be honest, I feared He could have spoken to me and it was a righteous fear (Psalm 111:10).

The Ancient of Days sat enthroned in His power and other thrones were put in place. His throne was a fiery flame and fervent steam issued forth from it, blasting out. An unnumbered host stood before Him (Daniel 7:9-11), and the Father reminded all present that He has given His Son dominion, glory and the title to the final Kingdom, in which all peoples, nations, and languages will one day serve. His dominion is an everlasting dominion.

A large angel cried out, "You alone are the Lord. You have made heaven, the heaven of heavens, with all their hosts, the earth and everything on it, the seas and all that is in them, and You preserve them all. The host of heaven worships You!" (Nehemiah 9:6).

Then, the morning stars sang together and all the sons of God shouted for joy (Job 38:7). Another cried out, "Bless the Lord, you His angels, who excel in strength, who do His Word, heeding the voice of His Word. Bless the Lord, all you His hosts, you ministers of His, who do His pleasure (Psalm 103:20-21). Praise Him, all His angels. Praise Him, all His hosts!" (Psalm 148:2-4).

The multitude of the heavenly hosts praised God, repeating the songs they sang on great occasions on earth: "Glory to God in the highest and on earth peace, goodwill toward men (Luke 2:13-14). For He has made us kings and priests to His God; to Him be glory and dominion forever and ever. Amen" (Revelation 1:6).

There were four living creatures present, which had eyes around and within. They each had six wings and they cried out saying, "Holy, holy, holy, Lord God Almighty, who was and is and is to come!" As they sang and praised, the twenty-four elders fell before Him who sits on the throne and worshipped Him who lives forever. They cast their crowns before the throne, saying: "You are worthy, O Lord, to receive glory, honour and power, for You created all things, and by Your will they exist and were created" (Revelation 4:8-11).

"You are seeing what was past, what is present and what is to come," the angel reminded me.

I looked again and beheld a great multitude which no one could number of all nations, tribes, peoples, and tongues, standing before the throne and before the Lamb, clothed with white robes, with palm branches in their hands, and crying out with a loud voice, saying, "Salvation belongs to our God who sits on the throne, and to the Lamb!" (Revelation 7:9-11).

All of heaven heard Him speaking forth His will, like the outbreak of thunder. There were also harpists playing (Revelation 14:2-3) and many sang the song of Moses, the servant of God, and the song of the Lamb, "Great and marvellous are Your works, Lord God Almighty! Just and true are Your ways, King of the saints" (Revelation 15:3-4).

Those around the throne continued to worship the Ancient of Days as He issued forth judgments for the times, seasons and the peoples and nations. I heard things from the past, present and for the future. He was righteous in all He spoke.

Those around the throne cried out prophetically, "Alleluia. Salvation and glory, honour and power belong to the Lord our God. For true and righteous are His judgments, because He will judge the great harlot who corrupted the earth with her fornication, and He will avenge on her the blood of His servants shed by her. Alleluia. Her smoke will rise forever and ever!" (Revelation 19:1-3).

Another voice thrust forth like a sword and fire mingled together saying, "Praise our God, all you His servants and those who fear Him, both small and great. Alleluia. For the Lord God Omnipotent reigns. Let us be glad and rejoice and give Him glory" (Revelation 19:5-7). Then the Lord thundered from heaven and the Most High uttered His voice. The earth shook and trembled.

The foundations of the hills also quaked and were shaken. Smoke went up from His nostrils and devouring fire from His mouth, coals were kindled by it. From the brightness before Him, His thick clouds passed with hailstones and coals of fire. He sent out His arrows and scattered the foe, lightning in abundance, and He vanquished them. At His rebuke, at the blast of the breath of His nostrils (Psalm 18:7-15). For there is nothing covered that will not be revealed, nor hidden that will not be known (Luke 12:2-3).

Chapter Sixteen

Hell

Instantly the angel pulled me away from the Ancient of Days and through the city. He began to tell me about the purpose of my visit.

"The reason for this journey is not for you to become self-centred, focusing on the blessings of your future, but to place a concern within your heart for the need of the lost to enter into Christ's rest. The Master came to seek and to save those who are lost (Luke 10:10), and all who are truly His will desire the same."

"If you speak of evangelism," I testified, "then I am not very useful."

"If you have a testimony of what God has done in your life," the man said, as he joined the conversation, "you can testify to others. Sharing the gospel includes sharing how faith in Christ's death and resurrection has changed your life. But there is more for you to learn because focusing on your own personal evangelism can also be self-centred. You are part of a Kingdom which spans around the world and you must be Kingdom-minded. People who care about the extension of the Kingdom of God do not feel concerned if 'their' ministry does not benefit from any labour, sacrifice and giving. Their focus is on God's Kingdom being extended and on the glory of its King. You must learn this because you can have an impact around the world, if only you would deny self to reach out and help another, who is evangelising those who have never heard."

"You know I cannot go to a foreign land," I said, as I took a stand.

"It is self-centred to believe that a call to help reach the world with the gospel means you must go," he answered. "If God sends you, then good, but think about this: Are you the only person who can testify to the nations? Why don't you think of others in their nations whom the Lord has already raised up? You could help local evangelists in their nations. Many are called to share the gospel with the lost that need your financial assistance. Why do you resist? The main problem you have is you still dwell in the shallow waters of your faith. You want to stay in the shallow waters because you can touch the ground and are still in control.

However, if you let the Holy Spirit lead you out into the deep, you will become a channel of His blessing to the world."

My experiences in heaven were not easy for my human mind to accept, because the flesh lusts against the will of the Spirit (Galatians 5:17), and the carnal mind is at war with the will of God (Romans 8:7, James 4:4). However, I was beginning to understand that unless my life changed due to these revelations, I would be in danger of self-deception. If I did not change my life, this experience could become another exercise in self-centred futile faith! I can imagine my carnal mind encouraging me to think: 'Comfort me with the hope of heaven and do not trouble me with the thought that many will not go there!' This is a terrible thing to think and yet my actions had confirmed I believed this for years, for I refused to think of the Kingdom around the world, and focused solely on my faith and the hope of my ministry. I had become spiritually 'fat' by feeding off Bible teaching and I had been unwilling to carry out any spiritual exercise to reach the world for Christ (1 Timothy 4:8).

"Do you know how you received the gospel?" asked the angel.

"Are you now seeking my testimony?" I replied hesitantly.

"No," he replied. "I am probing deeper than your lifetime."

Confused I turned to the man who had been silently listening and asked, "What does he mean?"

"There is a chain of grace reaching back thousands of years," the man informed me. "You can tell others of the person who shared the gospel with your family, and you can testify to the meeting when you first made a confession of faith... but go back in time, go back!"

"What do you mean?"

"Who built the church in which you were saved?" he said, as other questions followed. "Who shared the gospel with your father? Who shared the gospel with the preacher whom you prayed with? Who was the first evangelist to preach in your home town and bring the message to your area? Who lived sacrificially and gave so you could have this spiritual inheritance? Who gave up their lives so that Christian revival would break forth in your nation and revitalise the faith? Who was the first evangelist in your county? Who were the ones who followed that evangelist? Who was the first to bring the gospel to England? Who left the Middle East and North Africa to bring the gospel to northern Europe? This is the chain of grace that runs back two thousand years, and because of all of these and more, the gospel has arrived to you!"

"Wow," I replied, "I've never thought of it like that before."

"You must continue this chain of grace," he added. "Do you want your link to be the last one in your chain, or will you help others as they have helped you? Would you like to get to heaven and find people who were saved because of your life and sacrifice?"

"But," I protested, "I have already decided I will support at least one local evangelist in Asia. Why do you speak of this again?"

"You have no urgency of heart," the angel replied, "you have not seen hell and because of this, you are complacent. You have decided to help because you feel obligated, but you still resent having to make small sacrifices for the Kingdom of God."

The angel touched me on the back and I watched as time and space blurred around me, until I stood in the coliseum in Rome. It was filled with people dressed in Roman clothes and the coliseum appeared to be new. I sensed I was viewing history and I did not travel in time. The crowds were shouting out the name of a gladiator and I knew in my spirit that he was one of the most famous in history.

"Have you ever heard his name before?" the angel asked.

"Never."

He then began to communicate with me again, without words.

"Who was the most famous film star in 1932?" He followed this with two other questions. "Who was Britain's prime minister in 1928?" and, "Who was the richest man in America in 1926?"

I did not know the answers to these questions, yet my experience taught me that any question from God or His representatives is presented for my spiritual education.

I considered the questions and concluded that these people were once considered the most famous in their generation. The decisions of a British prime minister in 1928, would shape the lives of millions of people in Africa, Asia and the Middle East, and I did not even know his name. In 1932, the most famous film star would have been adored in Hollywood and the wealthiest man in America in 1926 would have been very powerful – yet I had no idea who these people were. A simple search could find the answer, but that was not the point. Most are ignorant of the lives of 'the once-powerful.'

Their world of the 1920s/30s had once seemed so powerful and everlasting, yet it all came to an end. Their glory faded so quickly. I now began to understand what the angel wanted me to know – life is short and we are quickly forgotten. Nonetheless, I comforted myself with the thought that many people's lives will continue to echo on in their descendants' memories.

The angel interrupted my thoughts and said, "Tell me the name of one of your great grandfathers" (Ecclesiastes 9:5, 1 Peter 1:24).

I was silent once again. My mind ran through my family tree and I drew a blank. I knew the name of one of my grandfathers, however his father's name I did not know. Suddenly I realised my folly! Did one of my great grandfathers comfort himself by believing his name would be remembered by posterity? His entire life has been forgotten by those whose lives rely on his choice to reproduce. I share a percentage of his genes and I know not his name.

"Vain and passing is the glory of all flesh," concluded the angel.

With that the angel touched my shoulder and I felt myself being pulled through the images of time. I was taken somewhere in the Middle East, hundreds of years before Christ's ministry on earth, and there was a great and mighty leader dying. Immediately I heard the voice of a prophet describing his life (and it also foretold Satan's judgment). The afterlife would not be kind to this powerful evil dictator whose life influenced many:

"Hell from beneath is excited about you, to meet you at your coming. It stirs up the dead for you. All the chief ones of the earth; it has raised up from their thrones, all the kings of the nations. They all shall speak and say to you: 'Have you also become as weak as we? Have you become like us? Your pomp is brought down to Sheol and the sound of your stringed instruments. The maggot is spread under you and worms cover you' " (Isaiah 14:9-11).

"You must see hell," the angel insisted.

"I am afraid," I testified. "There is nothing good in hell."

The angel took hold of my hand and we walked with the man, through the veil between the natural and the spiritual world (Isaiah 33:4). Due to my great concern about seeing hell, I knew I was only going to be given glimpses of hell in stages. So I was surprised to find myself, not in hell, for I was in a corner of heaven!

"You are to see what Isaiah witnessed," the man said, as he joined us. "You too will see the redeemed of the Lord go forth and look on those who have transgressed against God. For in hell, the worm does not die and the fire is not quenched (Isaiah 66:22-24). Jesus gave a three-fold warning of the endless fire" (Mark 9:44-48).

The angel led me to a cliff-edge where I could see down into hell and the inhabitants could perceive heaven (Isaiah 66:24, Luke 16:23, Revelation 14:10-11). I drew back immediately at the sight.

"You do not understand this," said the man, "but there are many victims of genocide and others who were victims of evil and unspeakable crimes; they died without witnessing justice. Now if they so desire, they will finally witness justice being carried out from this vantage point into hell."

"Please, may I leave?" I asked, as my hands began to silently tremble. "I now know why some preachers refuse to believe in hell," I concluded. "The reality is shocking. Sometimes man finds it easier to believe a lie because the truth is hard to accept."

"Some things will always be true, whether you choose to believe in them or not," the man insisted. "You must look and see. The Church has spent far too long avoiding this reality. For many hell is the truth seen too late (Luke 16:26-31).

"You can see into hell for a season. Look now and ask yourself these questions: Does the Church serve the peoples and nations righteously, when it refuses to warn them of eternal damnation? Is the Church culpable of gross negligence when it refuses to teach the whole counsel of God to believers and avoids its duty to warn all of eternal truth?" (Ezekiel 33:8, Acts 20:27).

"These questions are too hard for me to answer," I concluded.

"You must look and see for those who refuse to see," he insisted.

I slowly moved my body to peer over the edge. The first thing I heard was loud cries. It was a place of weeping and torment (Luke 16:23-28; Revelation 14:10-11, 20:10). I heard people shouting, hating and being hated. There were constant aggression and misery. There was no chain of command – no gangs, leaders, or friendships because each individual was isolated in a 'cell.' This is 'the blackness of darkness forever,' which Jude wrote about (Jude 13). In each 'cell,' one lonely individual was being tormented by the remembrance of his or her sins and by the sound of the misery.

They constantly felt the hate, anger and bitterness of all. It was a place of trembling; there were fears without and fears within.

"Who are these people in hell?" I asked the man.

"For this you know," he said, "that no fornicator, unclean person, nor covetous man, who is an idolater, has any inheritance in the Kingdom of Christ (Ephesians 5:5). These people once celebrated, joked and openly practised adultery, fornication and all promiscuity. They embraced uncleanness, lewdness, idolatry, sorcery, hatred, contentions, and outbursts of wrath – selfish ambition, dissensions, heresies, envy, murders and drunken revelries. They ignored the truth that those who practice such things will not inherit the Kingdom of God

(Galatians 5:20-21).

"Many you see viciously fought against the will and purpose of God for themselves and their nations (John 3:18). Look and see for there are also many who claimed to be Christian, and there are many who still wear religious outfits! They were religious by name, but behind closed doors, they were workers of iniquity. Their names are not inscribed in the Book of Life" (Matthew 7:22-23, Philippians 4:3, Revelation 22:19).

"What was the greatest sin of these people?" I asked (John 19:11).

"These are they that loved and practised a lie," replied the man, with a sad strain in his voice and a sigh (Revelation 22:15).

"What is the lie they practised."

"Jesus is the Truth," he replied, "and those who reject the Truth, will always live a lie" (John 14:6).

Hell is home to endless weeping and unquenchable fire (Matthew 13:30), and it was not just people who were there. I saw demons and various evil spirits of numerous ranks being tormented too. In their minds, they had memories of the glory and goodness of God, yet now they were paying the price for their sin against Him (Revelation 12:4).

I once believed that Satan was in charge of hell and his demons were responsible for tormenting people; now I knew this is a false idea inspired by my culture. For these demons had no power or authority; they were weak and trembled (James 2:19). These devils were powerless in hell (Isaiah 14:9-11).

"What does it mean when Jesus spoke of hell being a place of gnashing of teeth?" I asked.

"The gnashing of teeth is a sign of anger and rebellion against God," he answered. "Hell is filled with people who raged against Christ and His will. This is why many religious people will be in hell; they loved Him in words, yet by their deeds they raged against Him (Isaiah 29:13, Mark 7:6). When Stephen preached the people were cut to the heart, but they rebelled against the conviction of the Spirit and gnashed with their teeth against God's will" (Acts 7:54).

Hell has unbearable heat. The extreme heat manifested itself like the haze from an active volcano. The power of this heat leads to a great thirst for its captives (Luke 16:24).

"Why can't these people enter heaven?" I inquired with concern.

"They refused to feed on the Bread of Life and they refused the spring of Living Water that flows out of the belly" (John 3:18-20, 6:35, 7:38).

"If they refused these wonderful gifts from God, do you believe they should escape the judgment? Why did they despise the riches of God's goodness, forbearance and longsuffering? The goodness of God leads to repentance; but with hardness of heart they have stored up wrath, in the day of the righteous judgment of God, who will render to each one according to his deeds. Eternal life to those who continue in doing good and find glory, honour, and immortality; but to those who are self-seeking and do not obey the truth, but obey unrighteousness – indignation and wrath, tribulation and anguish, on every soul of man who does evil" (Romans 2:3-9).

The faces of people in hell were absent of any hope. In heaven, God has promised that there will be no more hunger, thirst, pain or tears. In hell, all the blessings of heaven are absent. They were all hungry and thirsty (Luke 16:24). They felt pain and were tired; there was no rest, both for the body and soul (Isaiah 48:22).

"Please tell me there is hope for them," I pleaded.

"Between us and them there is a great gulf fixed," he said, "so that those who want to pass from there to here cannot, nor can those from here pass to them (Luke 16:26). Now consider the words of Scripture: 'For the Son of Man will come in the glory of His Father with His angels and He will reward each according to his works (Matthew 16:27). I say to you that it shall be more tolerable for the land of Sodom in the day of judgment, than for the impenitent cities'" (Matthew 10:15), and he added, "Of how much worse punishment, do you suppose, will he be thought worthy who has trampled the Son of God underfoot?" (Hebrews 10:29).

"How will these punishments be decided?"

"For everyone to whom much is given, from him much will be required," he summarised, "and to whom much has been committed of him they will ask the more" (Luke 12:48).

"Does this mean there are various levels of rewards for obedience and punishments for sin?"

"The Lord said, 'Therefore the one who delivered Me to you has the greater sin' (John 19:11). He warned of judgment for misleading children (Matthew 18:6) and there are stricter judgments" (James 3:1).

The man showed me that the Bible has much to teach about hell. (Matthew 5:29, 7:13, 8:12, 10:28, 22:13, 25:30, 2 Thessalonians 1:9; 2 Peter 2:4, Jude 6-7, Revelation 14:11; 19:20; 20:10; 21:8). However, I had to ask him why some preachers teach it is not a real place. He showed me what Jesus taught in the gospels about hell and concluded, "Why do they doubt the teaching of Jesus?"

"They teach that God could never create such a place," I replied.

"God did not create hell for man," he answered. "Hell was prepared for the devil and his angels (Matthew 25:41), and by the testimony of Jesus, it is a place of everlasting punishment" (Matthew 25:46).

These words were profound and I stopped to ponder what he told me. He asked me, "Why do they doubt the teaching of Jesus?" This indicates that those who question the reality of hell, doubt the truthfulness of Jesus' teaching (1 John 5:10). How can Jesus be someone's Lord and be ignored like a liar at the same time?

I also realised it was never God's intention for anyone to go to hell. Hell was designed for the devil and his fallen angels, which cause so much misery for so many. Besides, the Bible teaches that God is a righteous Judge and love demands that a perfect sentence must be delivered. What kind of justice would there be if every offence went unpunished? Christ took the punishment for those who repent and accept His gift; yet for the unrepentant, their sins are not forgiven and they must be judged (John 3:18, 1 John 5:12-13).

As I thought about this the man said something which shocked me.

"Hell is the undiluted fulfilment of man's ultimate sinful desire."

"What is this desire?" I asked in puzzlement.

"Total independence from God," he answered (Job 21:14-15).

"Please help me understand this," I replied. "I am slow of learning."

"Hell is total separation from God," he stated (Matthew 25:41, 2 Thessalonians 1:9). "Those who reject Jesus and His purposes for their lives, forget they have been created in God's image (Genesis 1:26, Colossians 1:16). God is love (1 John 4:16), and all that mankind treasures in this life is merely a reflection of God. When you experience love, joy, peace, patience, kindness, goodness, faithfulness, gentleness and self-control (Galatians 5:22-23) – you experience God's character. This is the fruit of the Spirit of God. However, hell is the total separation from all that God is. He is love; He is Light, He is Truth, He is the Prince of Peace and the fullness of joy" (Isaiah 9:6, Matthew 25:23, John 8:12, 12:46, 1 John 4:7).

He summarised his description with this statement, "The absence of God is the absence of love," adding reverently, "Behold therefore the goodness and the severity of God: on those who fell, severity; but toward you, goodness" (Romans 11:22).

"Please clarify something for me," I asked with humility. "How would you describe hell in its simplest form?" His reply shook me. "Hell is the total absence of God and all He is" (2 Thessalonians 1:9).

The total absence of God is a shocking thought. God's goodness is revealed to us in His creation and in the love He placed within us (Romans 1:20, 2:12). Imagine a world where God withdrew all of Himself! The beautiful flowers would dry up, the vibrant green grass would wilt and die, trees would crash to the ground and the light would fail, leaving the darkness. I suddenly realised the truth, that all we love on earth is a reflection of God's goodness! Those who reject God and love the natural world are ignorant that they enjoy a reflection of God's grace in His creation (Isaiah 45:18). The ancients used to make idols of wood and stone to worship; today some still do the same by praising nature without acknowledging its Creator. They may not bow down to nature, but they do worship it ignorantly.

I never understood how much of God is around us at all times, even for those that do not believe in Him (Colossians 1:16). All the things we love about life and all the joys of nature are an expression of Christ. I had taken all this for granted without realising God is the true source – from a beautiful flower, a waterfall, to someone's sacrificial love for another. All this is from God and of God. Meanwhile, in hell – all this and much more is absent forever. God has withdrawn and all that is left behind is the carnal sinful nature, leading to inner lawlessness, wickedness, evil and rebellion.

There is an endless list of why hell is terrible. Those in hell had stored up wrath for themselves by their hard and impenitent hearts (Romans 2:5), and were subject to constant torment and fire. They were tormented by their own choices in life (John 12:48). In every minute they were reminded that they had rejected Christ. They could have been in the glory with God, in that place of total healing and rest. Yet they had mocked Him, laughed at faith in Christ's death and resurrection and called it foolishness (Matthew 25:3, Romans 1:21). Now in hell, they knew if they had only humbled themselves, they too could have been in glory. What a terrible thought to take captive of a soul for eternity. I thought about these things as we journeyed back to the city and then we talked about it.

Chapter Seventeen

Free Will

"God respects people's free will," the man explained. "Those who reject His salvation will be given what they want – a life without God. In hell, there is no personal restraint and self will consume self, leading to complete hopelessness. They will have nothing to live for and no hope for the future. Their carnal natures will consume them from within. Yet, they still rage against God. They want the blessings of heaven, but even if they were given the opportunity to submit to Christ, they would still refuse! They curse God even in death. They are of two minds. They want heaven, but not God."

"Even in torment, they are still raging against God," I exclaimed.

"Christ suffered and sacrificed all He had to save mankind," the man told me. "But He will not force people against their free will to accept His Lordship (Ezekiel 18:32, 2 Peter 3:9). Hell was prepared for the devil and his angels. Meanwhile, God prepared a Kingdom for man from before the foundation of the world. However, many will refuse to be a citizen of His Kingdom (Matthew 25:34). They are like the men Jesus spoke of who said, 'We will not have this man to reign over us' " (Luke 19:14).

"Some teach that everyone will go to heaven," I replied. "I do not doubt you; I'm just repeating what they preach."

"Do you believe that would be righteous?" the man asked.

I stood there silently, not knowing how to answer.

"Heaven is God's idea, it is His home. How can you reject God and plan to live in His home? If everyone went to heaven today – just as they are, all the problems of the earth would immediately be transferred to heaven! The unregenerate sinful and selfish nature would express itself, and paradise would be lost! Heaven would become like earth and the sins of man would destroy your eternal home. God would leave heaven because He cannot dwell with unrighteousness and heaven would cease to exist. Do you believe heaven should be the final home of practising adulterers, liars, thieves, murderers and so forth?"

How could I answer such a compelling argument? I decided to humble myself and let the truth penetrate my soul.

"You complain that you cannot go out without someone directing foul language at another," he told me. "Do you want to continue to live for eternity amongst angry and self-centred people?"

"We want to escape the wickedness of this world," I resolved.

"Only those who choose to receive Christ's total transformation of their soul and spirit can enter," he replied. "This is what takes place when we are united together in the likeness of His resurrection (Romans 6:5). He will forgive all their sins and He will transform them – and the destructive nature of the first Adam can never rule them or hurt another again.

"The greatest deliverance you can receive," he concluded, "is to be freed from self. On earth, you can choose to surrender self, yet the fullness of your deliverance only takes place as you are transformed into His likeness. Do not believe a lie – you cannot be a citizen of heaven and live for the desires of Satan on earth. For God did not call us to be impure but to live holy lives. Therefore, anyone who rejects this does not reject a human being but God, the very God who gives you the Holy Spirit" (1 Thessalonians 4:7-8).

In this revelation, I knew I viewed eternity through a glass darkly (1 Corinthians 13:12). So I had to be careful with my conclusions and my interpretation of what I was told. Nevertheless, I was left with the impression that in hell, the fullness of the grotesque nature of Adam is entirely expressed, as the image of God is removed from its human inhabitants (Genesis 1:27).

That nature described in Romans 1:28-32, overcomes the person from within; leading to self consuming self. This is the path to endless despair and it is self-inflicted. As those in hell choose not to retain God in their knowledge, He gives them over to a debased mind and they fill their hearts with wickedness, maliciousness, envy, strife, deceit and hatred etc.

In Paul's letter to Titus, he described how human nature leads to destruction; imagine how this twisted character would behave in a place where God's goodness is absent: 'For we were once deceived living in malice, envy, hateful and hating one another' (Titus 3:3).

Salvation from this self-inflicted destruction is only possible 'when the kindness and the love of God our Saviour towards man appeared...He saved us, through the washing of regeneration and renewing of the Holy Spirit, whom He poured out on us abundantly through Jesus Christ our Saviour' (Titus 3:4-6).

"I am worried that someone I loved may be in hell," I confided.

"This is a burden far too heavy for you to carry," I was told. "You must lay down all loves at the cross and put your faith in the righteous judgment of God (Matthew 10:37). He is very good, more than you could ever know. He has no pleasure in the death of the unrepentant (Ezekiel 33:11) and desires all to be saved (1 Timothy 2:4). When you trust in His righteous judgment, you can lay this question down and be free. The Judge of all the earth will do what is right (Genesis 18:25, Job 38-42). However, some want to go to hell to be with family or friends, but they forget that those in solitary confinement have no visitors and by grace, they may not be there!

"I can't help it," I replied, "I'm still concerned about those who die, who were not known to be in faith."

"Listen, son of the Lord. The burdens of eternity are not for you to carry. Trust in the goodness of the Lord."

Chapter Eighteen

The Kingdom of God

The man continued to instruct me. "Christ preached the gospel of the Kingdom and your generation has forgotten what it means to serve a sovereign monarch."

In Britain, the monarch is a figurehead, the embodiment of our values and laws, yet he or she is practically powerless. Power is exercised by men and women elected by the people. They make laws and wield power as they are guided by the will of the people, and the monarch – as Head of State – signs them into being.

Britain limited the power of the monarch with Magna Carta in 1215 and in 1689, the great powers of the monarch were dissolved as the English Bill of Rights led to parliament becoming supreme. It was these values that the English settlers took with them to North America and they are expressed in totality in the U.S. constitution.

"Many generations in the West have lived under democratic rule," the man summarised. "But the Kingdom of God is not a democracy. You cannot vote out parts of the Bible you do not like and the Holy Spirit will not abide with those who try to vote on His will (Acts 5:32). You have been called to serve a sovereign Divine Monarch."

"What does this mean in practical terms?" I inquired.

"In Bible days, a king was always born to rule and Christ was born in those days," he taught me. "The gospel of the Kingdom means the gospel of Christ's governance. This was the message that Christ preached (Matthew 4:23, 9:35, 24:14, Mark 1:15), and the people He spoke to knew that a king's rule is absolute. This is why James and John wanted to sit at Christ's side, for they wanted to rule with Him (Mark 10:35-37). In the prophecies of the Old Testament and the letters of the New, especially in the book of Revelation, there is ample documentation of the Kingship of Christ being exercised" (Luke 1:33, Romans 15:12, 1 Corinthians 15:25, Revelation 11:15).

"If you want to be a citizen of His eternal Kingdom you must accept His Kingship in every area of your life: 'For unto us a Child is born, unto us a Son is given...and of His government and peace there shall be no end' (Isaiah 9:6-7). One cannot reject His Kingship and be a citizen of His Kingdom! There is no room in heaven for rebels who want to undermine Christ's Kingship. If you want to be in His Kingdom, you must choose to accept His Kingship, because hell is the absence of the Kingdom and the King."

"Your teaching is complicated," I confessed.

"Then let this simple message drop down into your ears," he said. "Christ came to destroy the works of the devil and he who loves to abide in sin serves the will of the devil (1 John 3:8). How can you declare you are in God's Kingdom if you side with the evil one by continuing to celebrate the passing pleasure of sin? Righteousness is the truth and the devil resists all truth" (John 8:44, 1 John 5:17).

"But Paul was righteous and he struggled," I said (Romans 7:19).

"To battle against sin is a good sign" (Hebrews 12:4), "and Paul also wrote of the importance of renewing the mind (Romans 12:1-2). He encouraged all to renew their minds because the carnal mind can become a swamp of deceit, deception and falsehood."

"As I am a believer, how can my mind be like that?"

"You think and believe not what the Bible says, but what the world thinks and believes," he replied. "You have been groomed by your culture to believe that right is wrong and wrong is right (Jeremiah 4:22). You are a child of a generation which calls evil good and good evil (Isaiah 5:20). Their beliefs have become your beliefs. You think their thoughts and believe their lies. They have moulded you in their image and this is why your mind must be renewed."

"I have been in church all my life!" I said to defend myself.

"If I asked you a question, would you reply by the knowledge and beliefs of your culture or by your knowledge of the Bible? Would you forgive because God tells you to, or withhold forgiveness because your culture asks for justice before forgiveness? Would you tithe because you belong to the King or would you withhold because your culture is based on self? Would you cast out devils because Jesus commands you to, or would you deny their existence because your culture is blind to the spiritual world? Would you break curses and pray for blessings because this is biblical, or would you call that superstition because your culture has indoctrinated you against the Word of God? You believe more in your culture than in the Word of God. You have allowed your culture's ever-changing worldview and beliefs to shape yours – that should be resting on the rock, Christ."

"Is everything in my culture evil?"

"When your nation first sent missionaries out to foreign lands and people believed in Christ, they had to examine their own culture, and reject all that was against the Bible and God's view of the world. They once believed in many things and practised many cultural beliefs, but when Christ entered their heart they had to renew their mind to be conformed to a biblical worldview. Your missionaries told converts to examine their culture, their worldview and beliefs, and lay them at Christ's altar – now you must do the same.

"Today your culture has gone astray from a biblical view of the world and is far from God. Now you must examine your own beliefs and practices to weigh them by the standards of the Bible.

"Many in churches are seeking after wealth, success and honour in this life because their culture has indoctrinated them. Some have forced the ideals of the American dream onto the Bible and preach with that interpretation; they believe if they get 'those things' they will find in them, what they really want. However, if they searched the Scriptures they would find all they need in Christ. What they truly desire, veiled behind Satan's smokescreen, is peace and joy. This cannot be found in wealth, success or honour, but in Christ and by abiding in His perfect will. Even Solomon knew possessions cannot make us happy (Ecclesiastes 1:12-2:26), and yet God's people seek after all the things that the world seeks and believes their lies."

"Why have churches lost their way?"

"Many believers are lost in thought and deed because preachers have tried to make the focus of the gospel about this life. They have preached self-help, self-development and self-progression; yet the gospel has never been about this life! John preached, "Flee from the wrath to come" (Matthew 3:7). Jesus preached, "After all these things the Gentiles seek...but lay up treasures for yourself in heaven" (Matthew 6:20, Luke 12:30-34). Paul taught, 'If then you were raised with Christ, seek those things which are above, where Christ is...set your mind on things above, not on things on the earth' (Colossians 3:1-2). The gospel is not about this life, but the next. This life will one day feel like a half-remembered dream or a lost memory of decades ago; therefore focus your actions on eternity!

"You have learnt there are rewards in heaven," he continued, "and now I tell you in life, you will also reap what you sow (Galatians 6:7-9). A great number who call themselves 'Christian' are completely ignorant of the Divine principles and laws of the

Kingdom which shape their lives on earth and will define their eternity. If you do not forgive you will not be forgiven (Matthew 6:36-38); with the measure you judge another you will be judged (Matthew 7:2) and the accuser watches to spoil your abiding (John 15). The Bible is full of Divine principles for you to learn and follow, yet you and many others choose to remain ignorant of Divine law as described in the Bible!"

"What does this all mean?" I asked. "Help me see the truth."

"There are spiritual laws in the Bible," he told me. "Laws that define your life: If you forgive, you will be forgiven, give and it will be given to you, bless and you will be blessed (Luke 6:36-40), and so forth. These commands are given for your blessing and protection in the heavenly realms, but many are not blessed because they refuse to obey and without obedience, the blessing is withheld. You have much to learn. Do you believe you can live your life the way you want and remain ignorant of the precepts of Scripture? God's people are destroyed by lack of knowledge" (Hosea 4:6).

Chapter Nineteen

An Empty Soul

"No-one engaged in warfare entangles himself with the affairs of this world," the man told me (2 Timothy 2:3-4).

"What does this mean in real life?" I replied. "I am not a soldier. I do not fight. What is the battle you speak about?"

"We are in a battle," he replied. "The Kingdom of God is constantly clashing and plundering the devil's kingdom, and you are either a soldier in this battle or a victim of the war" (Matthew 11:12).

I was reminded again of Stephen's last sermon. He had preached by the power of the Holy Spirit, and the religious authorities fought against him and the glory of Christ. Then he saw into heaven. 'He being full of the Holy Spirit gazed into heaven and saw the glory of God, and Jesus standing at His right hand' (Acts 7:55).

Whilst Stephen was gazing into heaven the people fought against him and being filled with hate killed him (Acts 7:58-60).

"Why is the world filled with so much hate?" I asked.

"This world is still under the sway of the devil and evil functions best when no-one believes in it," the man declared (1 John 5:19). "When people live as Satan wants them to, it always leads to frustration and misery. One of the world's best-kept secrets is that God never asks anyone to do anything that is not eternally good."

"Where does the anger in the world come from?" I inquired.

"When people sin they receive the fruit of sin within," the man reasoned. "Therefore when people are always angry at others, it is often a reflection of the struggle within. The man at peace with God can be at peace with others and out of the abundance of the heart the mouth speaks. Their fruit will show" (Matthew 12:33-35).

"What are the struggles within man that you speak of?"

"It was revealed to James," the man stated.

"Where do wars and fights come from among you?" I read from the Bible. "Do they not come from your desires for pleasure that war in you? You lust and do not have. You murder and covet and cannot obtain. You fight and war (James 4:1-2)...If you have bitter envy and self-seeking in your hearts, do not boast against the truth. This wisdom does not descend from above but is earthly, sensual and demonic. For where envy and self-seeking exist, confusion and every evil thing are there" (James 3:14-16).

"Do you understand what he wrote?" the man asked.

"I need help," I pleaded.

"The world is self-seeking," he told me. "They lust for what they do not have and are prepared to fight with others for what they desire. This kind of self-seeking leads to being filled with anger, confusion and many other evils."

"At least the Church is better," I said with confidence.

"Do you believe that?" the man inquired. "Heaven is often clouded with the smog of selfish prayers, mixed with the selfless prayers of the saints (Revelation 5:8, 8:3-4). You always want something and you ask, not with selfless intentions, but selfishly. You want your prayers answered so you may spend what you receive on your pleasure, not for the Kingdom of God" (James 4:3).

"It is hard to walk the narrow path into Christ's will," I contested.

"I tell you a secret of great wisdom," he announced, "living the life is not the great burden people think it is – pretending to live the life is the heaviest burden. Imagine sitting by a spring of pure water and never being able to drink! How would it feel to be thirsty in the soul and to never have one's inner thirst quenched? The water of this world has no lasting taste, and you cannot drink of the spring of God and the world. This is the condition of every backslider in heart. They are close, but not close enough to drink.

"Jesus promised a spring of Living Water would flood from within the heart of those who abide in Him (John 7:38). He said, 'Come to Me, all you who labour and are heavy laden, and I will give you rest. Take My yoke upon you and learn from Me, for I am gentle and lowly in heart, and you will find rest for your souls. For My yoke is easy and My burden is light' (Matthew 11:28-30).

"Can you imagine being near the One who gives rest and never being close enough to have it? Never finding rest – what a burden!

"I tell you the truth, it is very costly to be near to Christ and not walk with Him. Those who 'play' at following Him pay a price in this world for His name, yet cannot claim any rewards or help from Him. They carry around unforgiveness, bitterness and strife within that eats at the soul. They battle with inner struggles and torments, yet they cannot be free because they are not walking with the Lord. They become spiritually impotent, unable to help themselves or others. What a travesty. Satan asks them to give up so much for so little. Oh, do they not long to be free?

"Some do not repent because they believe they cannot be forgiven; they forget that Christ weeps for them. They are Satan's prey; he harasses them and they do not know how to battle him or the world. What a miserable position to be in by choice! They are spiritually hungry, thirsty, tired, naked, wretched, poor and blind (Revelation 3:17). They cannot enjoy God and the world cannot fulfil them. They have seen too much of the light to enjoy the passing pleasure of darkness and they have enough truth to keep them convicted on all counts. The backslider is the prey of the unsaved and the lost sheep of the Church. They are not in one camp or the other. They are chastised by both, alienated from all. Inside is a constant war. What a conflict – with no peace, joy or hope.

"Oh to be free! How I wish they would choose freedom! Be free of the world and the chains of sin's consequences. Find liberty from the inner battle of fighting God and His will. Set yourselves free children of the King! Release yourselves from self-deception, and come to the Bread of Life and be filled" (John 6:33-35).

"You speak to me and others," I said, "but there are many Christians who are not free or happy."

"I marvel at people's ability to find unhappiness amongst such possibilities for spiritual abundance! You dream of another life and try to live vicariously through others in the media or elsewhere. Yet when you spend your life comparing it with others, you will despise your own. Millions are lost in self – discouraged and depressed. Dreams and imagination can accentuate life, they can't define it. This leads to darkness of the soul, when self consumes self. It occurs when all you can see is self and when your spiritual eyes have been overcome by the flesh. It is when self is enthroned above God's will. It takes place when you forget your responsibilities to Christ and seek joy outside of His Word. The more you look at self the bigger the mess becomes. Yet Divine love is the opposite of self, it is giving. God gave Christ and Christ gave all. It is sacrificial, free of all self-interest. Divine love is the crucifixion of self."

"We all need hope for ourselves," I said in defence.

"You need eternal hope in Christ," he testified, "for human hope will always fade. Human dreams sometimes come to pass and yet you still feel empty; whilst eternal hope will fill your soul."

"Then we will be happy," I exclaimed. "I love being happy!"

"Happiness on earth is circumstantial," he responded. "When your circumstances all come together as you hope, you may feel happy for a time. Jesus did not teach on earthly happiness, but joy. His joy comes when you abide in Him and His Word (John 15:11). Joy is a continual revelation beyond circumstances. Joy can be birthed in you if you stand in faith on the promises of God. When you fail to abide in God's will, your joy will disperse and when you stand on the Word and His promises you will walk towards joy" (1 Peter 1:8).

"Joy is a spiritual act of faith then?"

"You use your senses to connect with this world," he taught. "But there is another world, a spiritual world and you must exercise faith to operate in that realm. It is the Spirit of God who ushers you in by faith and the spiritual world is more real than your own."

"How can God's world become more real to me?"

"You can only experience His world by passing through the veil of Christ. You must exercise faith, and by faith enter into His death and resurrection. Listen to the Scriptures: 'Therefore, brethren, having boldness to enter the Holiest by the blood of Jesus, by a new and living way which He consecrated for us, through the veil, that is, His flesh, and having a High Priest over the house of God' (Hebrews 10:19-21). You desire much on earth. However, when a soul still feels hungry, it is because that soul was designed to find fulfilment in something they have yet to fully understand and receive."

"Do you speak of food?"

"You can stuff a hungry soul with everything worldly," he warned, "you can fill a life with money, goods and relationships. Yet it will not find true peace outside of an intimate relationship with God. It may be pacified by a distraction, yet it always passes. The world is not at peace because it is still searching. All the fights and anger derives from people searching in the wrong places, for what they think they want or need. What every person needs is to know God the Father through the Son, by abiding with the Person of the Holy Spirit."

"So, if we go to church we will be at peace," I concluded.

"No," said the man. "You confuse the church building with the Body of Christ. You should be the Church. You cannot go to what you are meant to be. You cannot find peace anywhere else but in the Lord Himself, by His Spirit. You cannot be sustained in and of yourself. You need an outward source of strength and that comes by the power of God operating in you by faith."

"Then, I will be happy?"

"No," the man said. "You must forget self to have God's joy. You must crucify the flesh. Christ died for all, that those who live should live no longer for themselves, but for Him who died for them and rose again (2 Corinthians 5:15). It is when you lose your life that you will find it (Matthew 16:25). This is what it means to be a new creation. When you forget self and live for His will and purposes, then the old will pass away and behold, all things will become new by faith" (2 Corinthians 5:17).

"You now speak of revival!" I indicated with a smile.

"Personal revival is always possible whenever people humble themselves and repent, to seek Jesus Christ in a fresh way – and then desire a fresh infilling of the Holy Spirit," the man confirmed.

"If revival can come quickly to us personally," I stated, "why has it taken so long for a national revival to take place?"

"Because God's people have yet to meet the conditions for revival," the man answered.

I was shocked by what he said and asked, "What conditions?"

"God said, 'If My people who are called by My name will humble themselves, and pray and seek My face, and turn from their wicked ways, then I will hear from heaven, and will forgive their sin and heal their land' " (2 Chronicles 7:14).

"I've been to many prayer meetings for revival," I said, "and we always mention that Scripture. We know it."

"You like to read it, but not fulfil the conditions," he warned. "You love self-seeking meetings. You love to invite famous preachers to come and make you feel good. You love to dance to music which encourages you. You love to invite famous worship leaders to lead you into songs to make you feel peaceful – but you don't like to humble yourselves in repentance, leading to a new life!"

"I enjoy meetings filled with celebration," I declared.

"How often is the focus of these meetings on self? The focus is often on you and what you want. You have prayed for revival; not because you want the lost to be saved, but because you have put your hope in revival to save you from the mess you have made!

"Instead of paying the price daily and living a crucified life you hope one big 'breakthrough' will deliver you from a lifetime of sin and rebellion. You want a miracle so you can avoid paying the price for personal victory. You want to catch someone else's anointing rather than pay the price for your own. You want a miraculous debt cancellation, rather than budgeting and giving up what you want. You want your body to be healed, and you still want to abuse your body by overeating and lack of exercise. If you received your miracle today, you would return to the same pit which you always dig, because your mind has not been renewed!

"One big breakthrough or miracle can never become a substitute for decades of spiritual slumber. You must pay the price in your own life for victory and when revival comes, you will be able to help lead others into victory. When God's Spirit is poured out again, will you be leading people to Christ or running for forgiveness yourself? When the Refiner comes He will search and test you (Malachi 3:2-3). Judgment must begin in the Church" (1 Peter 4:17).

"I do want revival," I testified, "I have prayed many times."

"You say your prayers without emotion," the man told me. "You read the Scriptures and do not weep. You confess out of obligation and rebel in your heart. You refuse to be broken."

Feeling challenged by these words I defended the reputation of the Church and myself, "The Church is good!"

"The Church must confess being lukewarm," he insisted. "It cares little for the Great Commission. It loves the gifts of the Groom, but does not want to be His pure Bride. It wants to be wedded to the world and Christ. The Church refuses to humble itself, pray and seek God's face. It refuses to turn from its wicked ways."

I was shocked by all I heard and did not want to ask any more questions on the subject. I had been to many prayer meetings for revival and now I was being asked some penetrating questions about our willingness to meet the conditions of 2 Chronicles 7:14.

"The Church refuses to be broken," he insisted, as I prepared to defend its record again. "Do not despair though – consider the churches of Revelation; how many of them were free of any rebuke? It is the same today" (Revelation 1:20-3:22).

"At least they testify of Him."

"They testify with their words," he said, "but what testimony do they share with their lives? The world can discern those who are genuine in their faith, from those who call Christ Lord and love the world. Do you not know that friendship with this world is enmity against God? (James 4:4). You testify with your mouth, but those you speak to see your works testify against you. They see you love the same things as them. They love the world and so do you!"

"I have failed to be a good witness," I confessed. "If God sends His glory to the Church it will change everything."

"God will not send His glory to any church which refuses to prepare for it," I was told, "because they will run from His glory when His holiness is expressed amongst them. Many who pray for God to move reject Him when He comes and call it counterfeit when it is different from what they wanted. They want it to take place as they desire, so they can control it for their glory. They want a 'clean' revival; and yet how many sinners enter the Church already clean! It is the sick who need the Great Physician (Luke 5:31). The Church should be a hospital where the sick can be made well; instead, it has become judge, jury and the executioner of sinners! Learn what this means: 'He desires mercy and not sacrifice.' The Lord Jesus did not come to call the righteous but sinners to repentance (Matthew 9:13). Before the world can repent, the Church must repent. Revival must come to transform the Church, glorify God, honour Jesus and allow the Spirit to move as He chooses and then the glory will spread."

"How will revival come if the Church refuses to repent?" I asked.

"Learn the lessons of history. God moves in power when He finds one or many human vessels through which He can express His holiness. Revivals have always begun when God finds one person, or a group who are willing to be broken and intercede in secret as they stand in faith waiting, no matter how long it takes."

"I wish more people would get saved in our churches now," I said.

"You wonder why the non-believer does not come running to your church," he determined. "The answer is simple. They do not come to your church because they came once before. They've already seen what your church has to offer in the power of the flesh. They came to meet God and found a carol service. They came to be healed and all they witnessed was false smiles and empty words on love. They came to find lives changed by God and they saw someone singing passionately, "I love you Lord," whom they knew as a wild drinker of alcohol with a promiscuous lifestyle. They witnessed 'the sacrifice of fools' (Ecclesiastes 5:1), devoid of real love for God and obedience (Numbers 30:2, 1 Samuel 15:22, Proverbs 10:19, Psalm 50:7-23, 76:11, Hosea 6:6). They wanted to find freedom from a life of strife, whilst they witnessed the hypocrisy of division, infighting and broken lives (John 13:35, Galatians 5:15). They came looking for people who live the truth and they found people living a lie. They came looking for acceptance and found judgment.

"There are many who live a lie," I was told (Amos 6:1, Revelation 22:15), "and they are being carried away by their own delusions (2 Thessalonians 2:11). One of God's judgments is to abandon people to their self-deception. He lets them live the lie they love.

"There are many deceptions from Satan," the man continued.

"One of Satan's greatest deceptions is to convince people that his path for their lives will not destroy them. His first temptation for Eve was to attempt to convince her that God was withholding something good (Genesis 3:4). Satan tries to convince believers that sin is good and they are missing out on many nice little sins. Yet the truth is that sin leads to destruction. God tells you to avoid sin because it will damage you – Satan comes to kill, steal and destroy (John 10:10).

"What is this destruction?" I asked. "I already know about hell."

"I will make it simple for you," he added. "On earth sin is mankind's self-inflicted punishment on all, for siding with Satan against God's will (John 8:44, 1 John 3:8). In this world SIN is your Self-Inflicted Nightmare (S.I.N.). Adam and Eve believed Satan and their sin led to a self-inflicted nightmare for all. When you sin, you may not feel the immediate consequences of it; yet as time goes on, what takes place? A self-inflicted nightmare. Why do millions despair in your world? Look around and what do you witness? Is it at peace? Does the world exhibit love? The further your nations have moved away from God, the worse they have become. This is your sin – your self-inflicted nightmare.

"You must repent and fully trust in Christ. He is the best friend anyone can ever have. He is the One who can save you from this nightmare, in this life and the next. God's way does not lead to devastation because the Kingdom of God is peace, joy and righteousness in the Holy Spirit (Romans 14:17). If you want to know what these are like, reject your sin and embrace the truth.

"Many believers need to listen to the rebuke of the unsaved. When they say to people, 'I didn't think you were a Christian,' it is because they have weighed their actions and found them wanting. How can darkness not be aware of the light?"

Chapter Twenty

The Cloud of Witnesses

"You have one more place to visit before you leave," I was told.

I followed the angel with the man. However, leaving heaven was the last thing on my mind and I didn't want my journey to end. My eyes were opened as I spoke to these two and I had learnt how shallow my faith had been.

"I don't want to leave heaven," I testified. "May I stay?"

"You don't want to leave because this is your real home," he said. "The desire for heaven has been planted as a seed into the soul of all mankind. They've always known within that there is a far better place because they've always desired it (Ecclesiastes 3:11).

"You want to live here now, but this is a selfish desire. You have a job to do on earth, to help others receive their citizenship of heaven. On earth, you can set your mind on things above and this mindset will help you to be faithful during your short time there. Your life is a vapour, it seems long to you, but it will end (James 4:14). Paul wrote that eye has not seen, nor has entered the mind what God has prepared; he also wrote that the Holy Spirit revealed it to them (1 Corinthians 2:9-10).

"The Holy Spirit will guide you into all truth (John 16:13), if you will receive Him as your Guide. If you meditate on the promises of Scripture (1 Timothy 4:15), the Spirit will give you revelation (1 John 2:27), and open the eyes of your understanding. This is why Paul prayed that the eyes of your understanding may be enlightened, that you may know the hope of your calling and the riches of the glory of His inheritance" (Ephesians 1:18).

"When I am on earth, heaven seems so far away and the cares of life are many," I confessed (Luke 8:14).

"You must consider your time on earth as the years of your schooling. They seemed endless to you and you felt powerless during those years. Yet, one day they came to an end. Those who chose to study hard at school spent their lives being able to reap the benefits of their choices; and those who rebelled and treated it all as a joke, regret their choices. In the same way, the choices you make on earth will echo in eternity and shape your everlasting life."

"How will my choices echo in eternity?"

"Once you enter eternity, there is no going back to start again and no second chance to do it better," he told me. "If you live selfishly you will have few rewards if you get to heaven and if you meet the conditions for the rewards you will receive them forever."

"Where does the Bible say there are no second chances?" I asked.

"Remember your Creator before the silver cord is loosed," he quoted. "The dust will return to the earth as it was and the spirit will return to God who gave it (Ecclesiastes 12:6). This is the curse of Adam which can only be reversed by Jesus Christ Himself: 'For dust you are and to dust you shall return' " (Genesis 3:19).

"I only have one life to live for God," I said in response!

"You must decide today whom you will serve, not only in word but in deed also" (Joshua 24:15).

"I have decided," I said. "I believe Jesus Christ is Lord. He died for my sins and was raised from the dead on the third day. He is now sat at the right hand of the Father."

"You were born again when you first repented and confessed faith in Jesus Christ (John 3:3-7). Now I ask, are you His vessel?"

"What does being a vessel involve?"

"Have you decided once and for all, that you will serve the Lord with all your heart, strength, soul and spirit? (Deuteronomy 11:13-16). I'm not speaking about ministry; I'm talking about giving God all you have and allowing Him to use it as He wills. I speak about giving the Holy Spirit the right to live in and through you, as He did with the apostles. Paul wrote that it was not him who lived in his body, rather it was Christ, by the Holy Spirit living through him (Galatians 2:20). He was crucified with Christ."

"How can I know if I am a surrendered vessel like Paul?" I asked.

"Who lives in your body?" he asked. "Is your entire life focused on fulfilling your will, your dreams and your desires?

"If the direction of your life is similar to a car journey – who is at the wheel driving and who is the passenger? Many people sit in the driving seat of their lives and take their vessels wherever they want. If they get into danger, they hope Christ will be ready to jump into the driving seat, to get them out of it. Then, when they are happy again, they want Him to leave or become a silent passenger."

"Can you explain this to me in a simpler way?" I asked.

"Are you free to go where you want, to live where you want and to spend your life with whom you desire? Are you free to work where you choose? Are you free to direct your money? Are you free to sin without conviction? Are you free to love the world and the things of the world? (1 John 2:15). If your answer is yes to any of these questions, you convict yourself that you are not a surrendered vessel of the Lord Jesus. You have sung, 'I surrender all,' and, 'I have been crucified with Christ,' whilst you keep all for self. You are not crucified with Christ and it is not He who lives in you."

"You are very challenging," I confessed. "May I go now?"

"This truth cannot be avoided," he told me. "For too long you have hidden behind religious duties. You have attended meetings, fulfilled religious observances, prayed and read the Bible; but have you allowed Christ to exercise His claim of Lordship in your life?"

"I thought to believe was enough," I said. "You should be pleased."

"Listen to the words of Jesus," he replied. "Not everyone who says to Me, 'Lord, Lord,' shall enter the Kingdom of Heaven, but he who does the will of My Father in heaven...Many will say to Me in that day, 'Lord, Lord, have we not prophesied in Your name, cast out demons in Your name and done many wonders in Your name?' Then I will declare to them, 'I never knew you; depart from Me, you who practice lawlessness!' " (Matthew 7:21-23).

"Who are these people expelled by Jesus Christ?" I asked.

"How many non-believers do you know who actively prophesy in the name of Jesus? How many people outside of the churches cast out demons and do wonders in the name of Jesus?"

"None I know of," I concluded.

"I give you a warning," he told me. "There are many former church members, preachers, elders and so-called 'Christians' of previous generations who are absent from heaven. They were not born again (John 3:3-7). They did not live for Him. They did not forgive and they were not forgiven (Matthew 6:14-15). They continued to practice lawlessness, whilst every week they attended a building and called it church. Many had a vague belief, whilst being backsliders in heart (Proverbs 14:14). Their fruit testified against them" (Revelation 3:5).

"I don't want to be lost," I pleaded. "Tell me what to do!"

"All must be born again," he stated. "All must repent and put their faith in Jesus Christ. They must pass from death to life (Romans 5:10, 24). Then afterwards all must make a decision, once and for all, to follow Him completely. Have you humbled yourself in prayer? Do you repent before Him alone? Do you confess your need? Have you wept the tears of a penitent soul before Him? Or are you still fighting Him and His will in every area of your life?"

"So few live this life," I declared. "Many are religious and few are sold out to Jesus; how can I stay on the narrow road?"

"You have the testimony of many in the Scriptures," he said. "Think of Peter. He did not vote on the will of God for his life. He did not challenge Jesus when He called him, or when He taught what a fully surrendered life would mean. Christ told Peter, 'Most assuredly I say to you, when you were younger, you girded yourself and walked where you wished, but when you are old, you will stretch out your hands and another will gird you and carry you where you do not wish' (John 21:18).

"When Peter was young he was free to do whatever he wanted with his life," he explained, "and when he accepted the call of God and the Lordship of Jesus Christ, he was led into a life that he did not plan or desire. Then, when Jesus ascended into heaven, it was the Holy Spirit who led him (Acts 10:19). He became a vessel for the Lord, and it was the Spirit who directed his life and purpose. Now, consider the testimony of Peter in his letters – did he regret his choice? No! Peter found more joy in serving the Lord than he ever had before when he was 'free' by the standards of this world. Today and for all eternity he has rewards in heaven."

"This is what Paul meant by being dead," I concluded. "He did not live for his desires, but for the Lord. However, this is not easy!"

"Giving up your life for Christ is like giving up a bicycle for a day and having to walk for a while – to be able to fly for eternity! Jesus spoke of the pearl of great price and the treasure in the field. These are the eternal rewards in Christ. Those who give Him everything are making a wise and eternal investment" (Matthew 13:44-46).

"Please speak words of ease and edification," I said. "Tell me I am to be blessed. I have been challenged too much!"

"Christians never cease to surprise me," the man concluded as he laughed. "You cry out in prayer to be closer with the Lord and you ask to go deeper with Him; and when He shows you the path, you turn away because of the cost! You focus on the temporal cost to follow Him, instead of focusing on the rewards He has promised. You desire to be the master of your own destiny and because you seek such, you refuse the will of the true Master. Have you considered your life outside of Christ's perfect will? You have been free to live your own life for many years, and where have your free-will choices led you? Are you at peace? Do you have joy? Do you have a purpose? Do you not sense that destiny is upon you?"

"You are right," I acknowledged. "I am lost outside of God's will."

"Listen therefore to the wisdom of the life of Christ," he told me. "For the joy set before Him, He endured the cross, despising the shame and now He is sat down at the right hand of God (Hebrews 12:2). If you are willing, you too could be given a privileged position with the heroes of the faith that abided in Christ."

I had been so caught up in this very challenging conversation, that I hadn't realised we had walked into a new area of heaven, and we were surrounded by people. We stood in a huge auditorium and in the middle there was a vast viewing section, where all could look down to earth. I looked and witnessed Christians working, praying, witnessing and serving the Lord. They had no idea they were being watched by me and others.

The view was extraordinary, and then I saw those who surrounded me and I was shocked. I recognised the faces of many! They all had heavenly bodies, and I knew them as the faithful Christians and preachers from the past. Some were famous and I realised I was staring at them.

"These men and women of God," he told me, "are part of the cloud of witnesses (Hebrews 12:1). Their lives are a witness to you of sacrifice, faith and perseverance; and the lives of believers are witnessed by them. They are the spiritual athletes of previous ages. Just like athletes who compete for a perishable crown, they too paid a high price to receive their eternal reward. In secret they pushed themselves hard, they had sacrificed and kept going even when it hurt (Hebrews 12:1-4). They trained, were faithful and now are rewarded publicly" (1 Corinthians 9:24).

In Hebrews 11 there are many testimonies of the exploits and faith adventures of the Old Testament heroes. Their sacrificial lives and tests of faith are mirrored in the cloud of modern witnesses, whose lives are documented in biographies, or by those who knew them. I sensed this cloud included people from Bible days to the modern-day, and it is an ever-growing number of believers whose faith exploits and the price they paid qualified them. To be a part of the cloud of witnesses is a very special honour and it is reserved for those who had been faithful and have given all to God.

I wanted to talk with many of those present and I gazed through the crowd to pick out faces of people I recalled from history. Some of these men and women of God spent thousands of years serving the Lord in heaven! They were as real and alive now, as they were on earth. Jesus testified that Abraham was still alive and rejoiced when he saw Christ's day (John 8:56). Abraham must have looked down from heaven at Jesus' ministry on earth!

The cloud of witnesses was filled with people who shone like the stars (Daniel 12:3) and I was struck by the fact that none regretted the price they had paid. None ever wished they had given less. To be here is a prized position and the entrance fee is exceptional.

I wanted to write down the names of the people I saw, yet I felt it was too sacred. Within my heart I was burning to speak to some of them, yet the angel spoke to me in my heart and told me not to. He concluded, "If you set your mind on the glory of living with Christ in heaven, you will be willing to endure all for Him" (Colossians 3:1-2).

On earth, we set our hope on many things and we are often disappointed. However, if we set our hope on the promises of God for eternity, then all the dreams He has put into our heart could be fulfilled. We are to live in a state of anticipation of all the good God has for us. This hope is an anchor for our souls and does not disappoint (Hebrews 6:19). It is this hope which provides us with a serene steady confidence in the ultimate goodness of God.

"God is a rewarder of those who diligently seek Him," he said (Hebrews 11:6). "God is faithful. For all the promises of God in Him are Yes and Amen, to the glory of God" (2 Corinthians 1:18-20).

Chapter Twenty-One

Number Your Days

"You must learn from the wisdom of Moses," the man told me.

"What is his wisdom?" I inquired.

"On earth, you number your years as they pass by," he stated, "but we number your days as they count down to eternity."

"How can this be?" I asked.

"Each day that passes on earth is a day you will never get again. Are you making the most of every day God gives to you? The wisdom of Moses is this: 'So teach us to number our days that we may gain a heart of wisdom' (Psalm 90:12). If all numbered their days by the implications of Scripture, most would expect (on average) less than 29,000 days for their entire life" (Psalm 90:10).

"I've never thought of living in such a way before," I acknowledged.

"Every day you spend in life abiding in sin – in anger, bitterness, unforgiveness, fighting and being consumed by self, is a wasted day," he insisted. "Each day you choose to spend in disobedience is a waste of the wonderful gift of God. It is only when you lose your life in Christ, you will find it – that was the message of the Master (Matthew 10:39). Today is the day to change! (2 Corinthians 6:2). You cannot return to live in the past, or go to the future; you only have now. You are living in the continuum of the present. Why waste any more time?

"Jesus did not leave you orphaned in your faith (John 14:18), He sent the Comforter, the Holy Spirit, to continue His ministry in and through you (John 15:26). Therefore you must welcome Him into your life, in the same manner you would if Jesus Christ was standing at your front door knocking to come in (Revelation 3:20). When you welcome Him to live in and through you, He will make you more like Jesus. Then as you read the Bible and your mind is soaked in God's Word, the Holy Spirit will bring to remembrance all the things the Master taught" (John 14:26, 16:7).

"Life is full of trouble," I insisted. "How can I live like this?"

"When you spend your life dwelling on the failures of the past, the pain of the present and your temporal troubles, you will lose sight of your heavenly future," he warned. "Troubles will come and you must endure by seeing the invisible (Hebrews 11:27). Faith is the invisible bridge you walk across to take you from the world you have known, to the world you will know. Faith will be the substance below your feet that carries you over the torrential rivers of life. It is the evidence which keeps your feet from falling and protects you from getting washed away in the river of despair (Hebrews 11:1). Then when the storms arise and sweep you into the rivers of life, faith will be the lifebelt around your waist, keeping you from drowning, and will allow you to be pulled towards safety."

As he spoke these things to me, I sensed I began to fade away from glory, like the moment in a dream as you feel yourself waking. I resisted this and fought by focusing my mind on the conversation.

"I don't want to leave the Father and the Son," I stated to the man.

"You are all to be a people for His possession," replied the man (1 Chronicles 12:18, 2 Chronicles 24:20, 1 Peter 2:9).

"I have no idea what you just said," I confessed.

"The Holy Spirit is God with you," he replied. "If you give your body, soul and spirit entirely to the Holy Spirit, He will fill you and you will experience what Paul testified: 'That you may be filled with the fullness of God' (Ephesians 3:19). Christ will live in and through you, as you allow the Holy Spirit to take possession of every part of your life. This was Paul's experience and he wrote of this: 'Christ in you the hope of glory' (Colossians 1:27). He will live in you and through you, when you die daily and let Him live His life" (1 Corinthians 15:31).

"I would love to walk with Jesus and talk to Him again," I indicated.

"You do not understand – the Holy Spirit is God on earth. He was sent from heaven to continue the ministry of Christ (John 14:16-18, 1 Peter 1:12). He should not be a silent bystander in the Church or in your life because He is God! He is the only living witness in the Church of Christ's death and resurrection. It was He who was sent to be your Teacher and Guide (John 14:26). He is the only Person on earth who knows and understands heaven. Jesus taught this:

"I tell you the truth, it is to your advantage that I go away; for if I do not go away the Helper will not come to you; but if I depart, I will send Him to you (John 16:7). When He the Spirit of Truth has come, He will guide you into all truth; for He will not speak on His own authority, but whatever He hears He will speak and He will tell you things to come. He will glorify Me, for He will take what is

Mine and declare it to you. All things that the Father has are Mine. Therefore I said that He will take of Mine and declare it to you" (John 16:13-15).

"This is new teaching," I stated.

"No," the angel said in mercy. "O foolish one and slow of heart to believe in all that the prophets and apostles have spoken (Luke 24:25); why do you continue to lack understanding? Have you not read the Gospel of John? He wrote in detail of the Lord's teaching on the ministry of the Holy Spirit. Jesus taught the Holy Spirit would continue His ministry in the Church (John 16:7-16). You must return and study John's Gospel chapters fourteen to seventeen."

"I want this relationship with the Holy Spirit to glorify Jesus," I testified, "but I do not know how to walk with Him."

"I have told you to study the Scriptures and you must," said the man. "Then you must surrender your body and will to Him. It is not enough for you to know His blessing or the passing shadow of His presence; you need to be filled with the fullness of God (Ephesians 3:19). Your body must become a container fit for His complete filling and habitation. When you give Him your will and invite Him to make Jesus your Lord, He will reveal Christ in you."

"It is a fearful thing to surrender one's life to another," I confessed.

"Not if the Person you welcome in is good," he replied. "God's good, pleasing and perfect will for your life will always be superior to your own (Romans 12:2). In the centre of His holy plan, you will find righteousness, joy and peace in the Holy Spirit. This is the Kingdom (1 Corinthians 4:20). This is why Jesus taught the Kingdom of God is within you. It is the change that takes place in your soul and spirit, as you wait for His heavenly Kingdom to come" (Luke 17:21).

"I thought to be a believer is supposed to be burdensome."

"Jesus taught, 'My yoke is easy and My burden is light' (Matthew 11:30). The everlasting burdens are the weight and consequences of sin. Consider your world lost in sin. Do you see light, joy and peace? Yet, the Kingdom of God is 'righteousness, joy and peace in the Holy Spirit' (Romans 14:17). These three blessings are all found in the Holy Spirit. If you don't have these, it is because you have neglected the Third Person of the Trinity. Jesus taught you need Him, so why have you not invited Him into your life in all His fullness? Many want His blessing and His power; how many want Him? He is the real treasure. He will take of what is Christ's and declare it to you (John 16:15). Give your life to Him, He is God."

"Your message is so different from what I hear from the pulpits," I contended. "How can I be sure this message is the truth?"

"Ask the Truth," the man replied (John 14:6). "Listen to what the Truth taught. 'If anyone desires to come after Me, let him deny himself and take up his cross and follow Me. For whoever desires to save his life will lose it, but whoever loses his life for My sake will find it. For what profit is it to a man if he gains the world and loses his soul? Or what will a man give in exchange for his soul? The Son of Man will come in the glory of His Father with His angels and He will reward each according to his works' " (Matthew 16:24-27).

"I want to serve the Lord Jesus Christ and be more than a pew warmer," I admitted, "please tell me what is my calling?"

"Have you ever considered that your desire for a calling comes from self? You want to know 'your' calling. Why are you the centre?"

"You continue to shock me with my root of self," I acknowledged.

"You want a prophet to pronounce what your call and destiny is! I know! However, your call is not to a destination or for a title. Your call and all who are followers of Christ is to walk closely with the Lord by the Holy Spirit. When you let Him live His life through you, then He will do the work of the ministry in and through you. He will transform you into His image and He will reach out to those whom He has chosen through you" (Acts 8:29, 21:4, Romans 8:29).

"Does this mean I have to wait and do nothing?"

"Some use waiting as an excuse to be lazy," he warned (Luke 16:10, 1 Corinthians 10:31). "Some will not lift a finger to clean their own home unless they believe God has spoken to them. Yet He spoke to them many years ago and they refused to hear His voice of conviction; therefore they will never hear His voice of direction."

"Please explain more of this to me," I pleaded.

"Before you can hear the voice of the Holy Spirit clearly in direction you must hear His voice in conviction and correction (John 16:8). He speaks to turn you into a vessel fit for God's will and when you respond, you give Him a reason to speak to you again in direction."

"How can I seek the Lord to do this?"

"You can seek the Lord and His Word daily, and you must give the Holy Spirit all you are," he insisted. "Have you invited the Holy Spirit to come into your life in all His fullness? When you do so, He will respond by entering and leading you to become fully dependant on Christ. When the Holy Spirit is your personal Guide and Teacher, Christ will be your Guide and Teacher (John 14:26, 1 John 2:27, Acts 8:29, 10:17-19). Remember God is One, do you abide in Him?"

"You speak awesome treasures to me," I declared.

"I speak what the prophets foretold and the apostles taught," he said. "When you have invited the Holy Spirit into your life to fill every area and you seek the Lord daily, then out of that deep relationship with the Holy Spirit, God will give aid to a needy world. Miracles and Divine appointments orchestrated by the Holy Spirit may well flow from your walk with the Lord. The miracles are not the walk – out of that close walk will come the miracles; if you seek miracles for themselves you will soon stray."

"Please send a prophet on the earth to confirm this word to me," I said.

"You want to receive specific guidance from a prophet," he replied, "and yet you have been called to be guided each day by the Holy Spirit (Acts 11:12, 28). Why do you seek the confirmation of a man, when you can have the inner confirmation of God? There are some who have heard the voice of a prophet and have rejoiced for a season. They had the fire for a time; however, they did not endure. Their fire was soon eclipsed by the call of the world. You must learn from their mistakes and endure in your faith. If you do not endure you will not receive your reward (Mark 13:13). Endurance is more than fire; it is the deep-rooted anchor within that will never give up!"

Chapter Twenty-Two

Mary or Martha

"Thank you," I said to the man and the angel. "I now know I have been called into the ministry, and it will feel good to stand in front of others and preach the Word to them. Those who once questioned my faith will feel very foolish when they see God using me!"

"Did you hear what you just confessed?" exclaimed the man. "You want to be in ministry to be seen by others! Instead of finding your worth in Christ, you want to find your value by what others say about you. Your inner confidence should come from Christ alone. Why do you seek man's approval?"

"I'm sorry," I said in humility. "I must consider all you say."

"When you invite the Holy Spirit to live Christ's life through you, He will reach out to others. However, be warned by those who have strayed from the Holy Spirit and still believe they serve Jesus. Many have been led astray to believe their 'good works' or 'ministry' is their relationship with God (John 6:63, Philippians 3:4). This is the work of the flesh and self-deception. They forget the wisdom of Mary and the warning from her sister's life. She too thought good works could substitute for sitting at the Master's feet.

"Jesus said, 'Martha, Martha, you are worried and troubled about many things, but one thing is needed, and Mary has chosen that good part, which will not be taken away from her' (Luke 10:41-42). The works of Martha were taken away, whilst Mary's faith lasts. The one thing that was needed by Martha was to sit at Jesus' feet in humility and to rest in His presence. The Master said, 'My sheep hear My voice' (John 10:27), and yet if you are part of His fold, you will need to be close enough to Him to hear His voice. If you draw near to God, He will draw near to you' " (James 4:8).

"I'm confused," I conceded. "Are we all called to official 'full-time' Christian ministry? Like a preacher, evangelist or missionary?"

"The pulpit is not the destination," he told me. "Many, oh, so many have become 'so busy' with the ministry, and yet there is little fruit of the Spirit in their lives and little fruit from their labour. They have not heeded the warning of Martha as they sought

God's approval by good works. Heed my warning; good works can still be works of the flesh. Jesus taught, 'That which is born of the flesh is flesh and that which is born of the Spirit is spirit' (John 3:6). If the ministry did not begin by the Spirit of God, then it began in the flesh and those who laboured will suffer loss in the judgment" (Matthew 15:13, 1 Corinthians 3:15). Your generation is addicted to Martha's ministry and rejects the simplicity of Mary's abiding faith."

"How can we know the difference between wearing ourselves out, thinking we are serving God, from literally doing His will?"

"You should not seek the call, but the One who calls. The call is to become one with Him by the Spirit of Truth. Too many have become lost in ministry. They have become too busy to see or hear from the Lord and they have no time to learn to become sensitive to the Holy Spirit. They are lost in self, lost in their ministry, lost in their works and lost in life.

"True ministry begins when you give yourself entirely to the Spirit and allow Him to lead you in the paths of Christ. This kind of ministry only takes place when the Holy Spirit leads you to fulfil God's will and it will always consume your life. The apostles were led by the Holy Spirit into Christ's perfect will (Acts 8:29, 39, 10:19, 13:2, 16:6-7). However, you must learn that preaching, teaching and exhortation are not the fulfilments of ministry. The five-fold ministries are given 'for the equipping of the saints for the work of ministry' (Ephesians 4:12). The equippers are servants called by God to serve believers and to prepare them for the work of reaching the world with Christ. The proof that the five-fold equippers are fulfilling their purpose can be found when the saints are doing the work of God. Every Christian is called to serve the Lord!"

"How can normal Christians do the work of God?" I asked.

"When they surrender their lives to the Holy Spirit He will guide them. He will be the One doing the ministry. Nevertheless, here is a warning for those who have ears to hear. He who begins in the Spirit must continue in the Spirit. Are you prepared to learn from the mistakes of others?

"Many have begun a work as the Lord has directed them, and yet when troubled times came, or the testing of the wilderness tried them they gave up. Others were deceived by well-meaning untested and unaccountable believers, or by false advisors sent by the devil. As these people stopped listening to the leading of the Holy Spirit, the work went astray and the power of the flesh took over. In these moments the Lord often withdraws to test His servants to see what is in their heart (1 Chronicles 21:1, Psalm

66:10, Jeremiah 12:3, Hebrews 11:17, Revelation 3:18). When these people neglect to continue in the Spirit, they listen to many other voices and the work is led astray. For others, the ministry collapses, shrinks or even grows, as the work is diverted from its original intent to become a consuming monster, which constantly needs to be fed. The tail begins to wag the head. Many good people have fallen into this trap of the enemy. They started as a Mary but ended up a Martha.

"Nevertheless, for most the greatest concern is the self-deception of the heart. How people want to be seen to be doing! Many believers want someone to give them the key to a pulpit or a ministry position and title. They want others to recognise and promote them and it becomes all 'about their ministry.'

"Why trust in the power of the flesh? Surrender to the Holy Spirit and let Him lead you into His ministry instead. You cannot reach the lost by preaching to the saved. Whenever He leads you to love, it will open a door to reach someone who has never been reached."

"I don't know this walk," I said with sadness. "I know so little of hearing the voice of God and walking with the Holy Spirit."

"Listen to the testimony of the apostles. Did Philip seek someone's ministry, or did the Spirit lead Him into His ministry? Consider this: 'Then the Spirit said to Philip, "Go near and overtake this chariot" ' (Acts 8:29). What of Peter? Did he seek for a human being to give him a ministry, or did he rely entirely on the Holy Spirit to reach out to the world through him? Read and ponder this: 'While Peter thought about the vision, the Spirit said to him, 'Behold, three men are seeking you. Arise therefore, go down and go with them, doubting nothing; for I have sent them' (Acts 10:19-20).

"Did Paul call himself or did the Holy Spirit send him? Find your answer in these words: 'As they ministered to the Lord and fasted, the Holy Spirit said, "Now separate to Me Barnabas and Saul for the work to which I have called them" ' (Acts 13:2).

"The Holy Spirit truly was their Guide into God's will," I declared.

"These testimonies are the result of years of obedience, faith and sacrifice. Peter had years of training with Jesus and Paul went into the deserts of Arabia to learn to abide with God (Galatians 1:17). They all learnt to be sensitive to the Holy Spirit and obeyed Him when He led them. In the silent years of testing and open trial, they became completely dependant upon Him. They obeyed when He sent them out and when He forbade them, they continued to obey. Dwell on this testimony: 'Now when they had gone through Phrygia and the region of Galatia, they were forbidden by the Holy Spirit to preach the word in Asia. After they had come to Mysia, they tried to go into Bithynia, but the Spirit did not permit them' " (Acts 16:6-7).

"These Scriptures are a great encouragement to me; however these people lived long ago," I protested. "Are there no examples from the modern world?"

"There are many unseen that live this life," he told me, "and often it is after they have left this world, that the Lord allows their stories to be told. You do have testimonies of people who have lived this life."

"Who are these people?" I inquired. "Please help me."

The angel lifted his hand and signalled for me to turn around. I did so and there standing in front of me was Rees Howells and his son Samuel Rees Howells! These men had lived like the prophets of the Old Testament and were powerful intercessors for the nations. The intercession of the Holy Spirit in them (Romans 8:26, Ephesians 3:10), had a major role to play in shaping twentieth century history, in the same way as the prophets of old.

Both men looked strong, confident in the Lord and were in the best of health. Surprisingly, I saw them in their human physical form, though they were spiritual. Rees Howells appeared to be in his early-fifties and was strong in vigour. He looked as he did before the deep and costly intercessions of WWII that shattered his health. Samuel Rees Howells appeared about forty-five years old with the strength of youth, like he was before the intercession for the demise of Communism and the Soviet Union came upon him.

I believe these men were shown to me to encourage me to live for Christ alone, as they did by giving themselves completely to the Holy Spirit to serve Jesus (John 16:13-15).

"If you want to know the Holy Spirit as they did," the man said, "you must obey Him as they did. He first speaks in whispers as He convicts of sin and guides you to righteousness. Then, if you listen to Him, He shall speak again and guide you into God's will for you."

"I once heard the Spirit in my church many years ago," I said.

"In many churches, God has been squeezed out of the meetings. The Spirit was welcome to speak for a season in some churches, yet He was silenced by those who became complacent (Amos 6:1). He spoke decades ago and people rejoiced, and then they chose not to listen carefully to what He said and ignored His messages. He convicted people of sin and they hardened their hearts. He gave direction and they became content with routine. He showered His gifts on them and they played with them. They asked for a prophet and they were happy to be blessed by his words of encouragement, but they shut their ears when he spoke words of rebuke or direction. They called out for an intercessor and they loved it when he prayed for what they wanted; yet they were offended when he wept tears of repentance and abided in God's presence for hours, upsetting their routine. The Holy Spirit does not choose to be silent, He is ignored. These words summarise why — disobedience and rebellion."

"You shock me once again," I confessed.

"Jesus said, 'If you love Me, you will obey Me.' What else does the Church need to know? If the local church loved Christ, it would obey Him and if it does not love Him, it will not obey (John 14:15, 15:14). Your words and songs declare so much, but they testify against you. Will you heed the warnings of the Lord? He said, 'Out of your own mouth I will judge you' " (Luke 19:22).

I then fell to my knees and cried out, "I am a sinful man, please send me away (Luke 5:8). You do not speak of others only, but me!"

"Two men went to prayer," the man replied, "one was a religious man who thanked God he was not an adulterer or a thief. He tithed, attended worship and was given to fasting. The other was a sinner who dared not look up to heaven, and he bowed his head in repentance and asked for mercy. On his knees, he wept saying, 'God be merciful to me a sinner' (Luke 18:9-14). The person God forgave was not the religious man in his pride, but the humble sinner. There are many 'Christians' filled with pride who will be judged and God hates religious arrogance" (Matthew 23:13-34).

"Heed the warning of the Lord," he added. "Why do you call Me, 'Lord, Lord,' and not do the things which I say? Whoever comes to Me, and hears My sayings and does them, I will show you whom he is like: He is like a man building a house, who dug deep and laid the foundation on the rock. And when the flood arose, the stream beat vehemently against that house, and could not shake it, for it was founded on the rock. But he who heard and did nothing is like a man who built a house on the sand without a solid foundation, against which the stream beat vehemently; and immediately it fell. And the ruin of that house was great" (Luke 6:46-49).

"Help me build my life on the rock Christ Jesus," I cried out.

"The Lord said, 'Behold I stand at the door and knock' (Revelation 3:20). However, He was not standing at the door of the unbelievers' heart, but at the door of the believers' heart and of the Church!"

"I am amazed," I said with wonder, as the angel lifted me onto my feet. "Christ stands at the door of the Church and the heart of believers, including mine, asking to come in!"

"Yes," said the man, "and He is still stood outside knocking and if you open the door to Him, you will find not the physical presence of Jesus (for you know He is at the right hand of the Father), but you will find the Spirit of Christ – the Holy Spirit" (Romans 8:9).

"So if I reject the Spirit of God," I replied, "I am rejecting Jesus."

"The Spirit and Jesus testified together that Christ stands at the door knocking!...'Behold, I stand at the door and knock, if anyone hears My voice and opens the door, I will come in to him and dine with him and he with Me...He who has an ear, let him hear what the Spirit says to the churches' (Revelation 3:20-22).

"Do you realise that in all eternity, these last day generations will be remembered as the people who had the most, yet did the least with all the talents God gave them? (Matthew 25:14-30). With all your wealth, gadgets and tools for communication, you still have not shared the gospel with the world! You get excited about filling your pockets with money, products and new gadgets, but have little desire to join the angels to celebrate as souls get truly born again. The true treasure of your heart is found in what you spend your time, money and effort pursuing. Do you pursue God's will or your will?

Chapter Twenty-Three

Unbelief and Denial

My two guides on this journey then whispered to me that the time of my departure had come. The man also warned me that two demons had been sent to harass me after I departed.

"The spirits of unbelief and denial have been sent by the enemy to suppress your faith," he warned. "They desire to drop ideas into your mind and whisper doubts to you, in an attempt to make you think their thoughts. They want you to deny all you have seen and heard and will encourage you not to believe. You have the power to resist them and to cast devils off you and out (Mark 16:17). You must battle them and deny their lies" (John 8:44).

"How can I fight them?"

"If your mind is empty, void of the Word and testimony of God, they can place their ideas and thoughts into your mind. This is one of the reasons that Paul wrote you must dwell on what is pure, holy and good (Philippians 4:8); for a mind filled with God cannot become the dumping ground of the enemy" (1 Timothy 4:5).

"What should I think?"

"The Lord instructed Joshua: 'This Book of the Law shall not depart from your mouth, but you shall meditate on it day and night, that you may observe to do according to all that is written in it. For then you will make your way prosperous and then you will have success. Have I not commanded you? Be strong and of good courage; do not be afraid, nor be dismayed, for the Lord your God is with you wherever you go' " (Joshua 1:8-9).

"I have many doubts," I confessed.

"You must believe your beliefs and doubt the doubts from devils. These attacks of the enemy are not new to you (1 Peter 5:8), and if you choose to abide in unbelief instead of faith, they will win. In the past you listened to their lies, instead of abiding in the truth. Now you must allow the Spirit to wield His sword."

"This is a difficult saying to understand," I replied.

"Dwell on this and you will learn the path to victory," he insisted. "Jesus is the Word and the Word of God is the sword of the Spirit (John 1:1, Ephesians 6:17, Hebrews 4:12). You know Jesus, or rather you are known by Him (Galatians 4:9); now you must get to know the One who yields His sword – the Holy Spirit."

As the angel said this to me, he stepped closer and hugged me goodbye. I was amazed at his embrace and it prompted a question.

"Does this mean we are friends?"

"We have always been friends in Christ," he replied, "and a true friend will speak the truth in love. As iron sharpens iron, so I have sharpened your faith (Proverbs 27:17). A true friend will be honest about heaven and hell, and will help you see your hypocrisy and self-deception. Open rebuke will always be better than hidden love (Proverbs 27:5). However, I know that many believers are not able to give a loving rebuke, because they speak in pride, arrogance and in a spirit of revenge. Only those with a broken heart can be trusted with giving a loving rebuke."

"You have been found faithful," I told the angel. "I have feared you on this journey and you have been stern. Yet your honesty has helped to provoke a change in my life and has enabled me to see all in a new light; the light of heaven!"

"Now you have seen this revelation and had your eyes opened to your weakness, go back and live with eternity in your heart," he replied. "Change your ways and do all you can to reach the world with the gospel. Do not become a lost link in His chain of grace."

"Thank you for being a true friend," I told the angel. I smiled within myself at this conclusion to my trip. I had struggled with the angel and yet what a true friend he became (Ephesians 4:15).

"Thank you for comforting me and understanding my faults," I said to the man who also helped me. "You have guided me with care, compassion and courage. You have answered my questions, even when they were the words that sprung from a blinded heart."

"We will see each other again," the angel replied.

"I look forward to meeting you again in heaven," I cried out, as I faded further away towards earth.

"No," said the angel, "we will meet again when you are drawn again into the heavenly realms! This revelation of heaven is the first part of a far greater revelation!"

I should have been overwhelmed by his words, as I now knew this was not the last revelation I would receive. However, a deep sleep came upon me and I found myself drifting between the veil that separates heaven from earth. It is a spiritual barrier that man cannot see and heaven began to be transparent in my eyes.

As the man faded away, I also saw the evil spirits that the angel warned me about, coming near. They were puny in presence, yet their words seemed powerful and their speech appeared as darts of unbelief. They threw them at me and their deadly poison was released into my thoughts.

I awoke later, and my mind became overwhelmed with doubt, confusion and unbelief. Suddenly I realised what was happening! I was told that unbelief and denial would come after me, and they would try to make me think their thoughts. This was now happening! An invisible enemy was attacking my mind and was throwing unseen darts of doubt, unbelief and denial. They wanted me to think these were my thoughts, but they were their doubts.

"I bind you evil spirits in the name of the Lord Jesus Christ," I declared. "Jesus Christ is Lord! I believe in the Father, Son and the Holy Spirit. Christ is victorious and He has defeated the enemy."

However, the thoughts kept coming and I did not know what to do. Then from within, I heard a voice speaking and putting new thoughts into my mind. "You must use the sword of the Spirit and the shield of faith to extinguish the fiery darts of the devil" (Ephesians 6:16-17).

I then began to read out Scriptures about Christ's complete victory over the enemy and a wave of peace within flooded my soul. I finished my declarations of faith with: "I plead the victory of the blood of Jesus Christ. Jesus is Lord; He is the Son of God and the Saviour of the world. All unbelief must be gone because He has delivered me from the Kingdom of darkness and transferred me to the Kingdom of the Son of His love (Colossians 1:13). He has disarmed principalities and powers of darkness, and made a public spectacle of them, triumphing over them by the cross (Colossians 2:15). And they overcame him by the blood of the Lamb and by the word of their testimony, and they did not love their lives to the death (Revelation 12:11). Thanks be to God who gives us the victory through our Lord Jesus Christ" (1 Corinthians 15:57).

As I finished declaring these truths from Scripture, the darts of the enemy fell from my mind and the devils fled until an opportune time for another attack (Luke 4:13).

"You are wielding My sword," said the Voice from within and I knew it was the Holy Spirit (Acts 10:19). I was back on earth and I could not speak with the angel or the man. Therefore, I now had to learn to know the voice, guidance and the abiding presence of the Third Person of the Trinity.

"I am the Comforter," He whispered. "I have come to be your Teacher and Guide (John 16:13). I will bring to remembrance all

Jesus taught and I will glorify Him (John 14:26, 16:14). Do you remember these words of Christ?

"In My Father's house there are many mansions...I go there to prepare a place for you" (John 14:2).

To be continued in *The End Times* by Paul Backholer.

ByFaith Media Books

Revival Fires and Awakenings – Thirty-Six Visitations of the Holy Spirit by Mathew Backholer.

Reformation to Revival, 500 Years of God's Glory: Sixty Revivals by Mathew Backholer

How to Plan, Prepare and Successfully Complete Your Short-Term Mission by Mathew Backholer.

Revival Fire – 150 Years of Revivals by Mathew Backholer documents twelve revivals from ten countries.

Discipleship for Everyday Living by Mathew Backholer. A dynamic biblical book for Christian growth.

Global Revival, Worldwide Outpourings, Forty-Three Visitations of the Holy Spirit by Mathew Backholer.

Understanding Revival and Addressing the Issues it Provokes by Mathew Backholer.

Extreme Faith – On Fire Christianity by Mathew Backholer. Powerful foundations for faith in Christ!

Revival Answers: True and False Revivals by Mathew Backholer. What is genuine and false revival?

*Short-Term Missions, A Christian Guide to STMs, For Leaders, Pastors, Students…*by Mathew Backholer.

Budget Travel, A Guide to Travelling on a Shoestring Explore the World, A Discount Overseas Adventure Trip: Gap Year, Backpacking by Mathew Backholer

Prophecy Now, Prophetic Words and Divine Revelations, For You, the Church and the Nations by Michael Backholer.

Samuel Rees Howells: A Life of Intercession by Richard Maton. Learn how intercession and prayer changed history.

Samuel, Son and Successor of Rees Howells by Richard Maton. Discover the full biography of Samuel Rees Howells.

The Holy Spirit in a Man by R.B. Watchman. An autobiography.

Tares and Weeds in your Church: Trouble & Deception in God's House by R.B. Watchman.

How Christianity Made the Modern World by Paul Backholer.

Holy Spirit Power: Knowing the Voice, Guidance and Person of the Holy Spirit by Paul Backholer.

The Exodus Evidence In Pictures – The Bible's Exodus by Paul Backholer. 100+ colour photos.

The Ark of the Covenant – Investigating the Ten Leading Claims by Paul Backholer. 80+ colour photos.

Jesus Today, Daily Devotional: 100 Days with Jesus Christ by Paul Backholer.

Britain, A Christian Country by Paul Backholer.

Celtic Christianity and the First Christian Kings in Britain by Paul Backholer.

The Baptism of Fire, Personal Revival and the Anointing for Supernatural Living by Paul Backholer.

Lost Treasures of the Bible by Paul Backholer.

The End Times: A Journey Through the Last Days. The Book of Revelation by Paul Backholer.

Christianity Rediscovered: In Pursuit of God and the Path to Eternal Life by Mathew Backholer.

God Challenges the Dictators, Doom of the Nazis Predicted by Rees Howells and Mathew Backholer

ByFaith Media DVDs

Great Christian Revivals on 1 DVD is an uplifting account of some of the greatest revivals in Church history. Filmed on location across Britain and drawing upon archive information, the stories of the Welsh Revival (1904-1905), the Hebridean Revival (1949-1952) and the Evangelical Revival (1739-1791), are told in this 72 minute documentary.

ByFaith – Quest for the Ark of the Covenant on 1 DVD. Experience an adventure and investigate the mystery of the lost Ark of the Covenant! Explore Ethiopia's rock churches; find the Egyptian Pharaoh who entered Solomon's Temple and search for the Queen of Sheba's Palace. Four episodes. 100+ minutes.

ByFaith – World Mission on 1 DVD. Pack your backpack and join two adventurers as they travel through 14 nations on their global short-term mission (STM). Get inspired for your STM, as you watch this 85 minute adventure; filmed over three years.

Israel in Egypt – The Exodus Mystery on 1 DVD. A four year quest searching for the evidence for Joseph, Moses and the Hebrew Slaves in Egypt. Explore the Exodus route, hunt for the Red Sea and climb Mount Sinai. This is the best of the eight episode TV series *ByFaith – In Search of the Exodus.* 110+ minutes.

ByFaith – In Search of the Exodus on 2 DVDs. The quest to find the evidence for ancient Israel in Egypt, the Red Sea and Mount Sinai, in eight TV episodes. 200+ minutes.

Visit **www.ByFaith.org** to find these DVDs and search for 'Paul Backholer Documentaries' on streaming services.

www.ByFaithDVDs.co.uk

Notes

Notes

Lightning Source UK Ltd.
Milton Keynes UK
UKHW020617170520
363290UK00009B/773